The Ultimate Guide to Self-Regulation for Parents

From Reactive to Mindful Parenting. Simple Strategies to Manage Emotions, Enhance Parental Skills, and Nurture Emotionally Intelligent Children

Claudia Turcotte

Contents

Introduction ... 1

1. The Foundation of Self-Regulation ... 5

2. Identifying and Understanding Personal Triggers ... 15

3. Strategies for Emotional Regulation ... 29

4. Communication that Connects ... 45

5. Establishing a Positive Family Dynamic ... 57

6. Daily Practices for Self-Regulation ... 73

7. Addressing Specific Challenges with Self-Regulation ... 83

8. Self-Care for Parents ... 101

9. Sustaining Growth and Embracing Change ... 113

Conclusion ... 123

About the author ... 129

Introduction

One hectic morning, as I scrambled to prepare breakfast, mediate sibling squabbles, and find missing shoes, I caught a glimpse of my reflection in the kitchen window. The furrowed brow and tight lips were all too familiar. In that frazzled reflection, I realized the need for a change—not just for the sake of my schedule, but for my soul and the little eyes watching how I handle stress. This chaotic moment marked the beginning of my transformative journey and served as the starting point for our exploration into mindful parenting.

This book is rooted in a simple yet profound truth: effective parenting is rooted in the parent's ability to self-regulate. The way we manage our emotions lays the groundwork for our family dynamics and directly influences our children's psychological and emotional well-being.

My vision for this book is crystal clear—to equip you with practical, actionable strategies that foster self-regulation and mindful parenting. By engaging with these pages, you will discover practical ways to better navigate your emotions, enhance your parenting approach, and, ultimately, strengthen your family connections. These strategies are not just theoretical concepts but tried and tested methods that you can confidently apply in your daily life, empowering you to take control of your parenting journey. Take the time to explore these strategies, discern what resonates with you, and implement those elements into your life at a pace that feels comfortable for you and your family.

My journey from a self-confessed 'control freak' mom to a more present, calm parent has been transformative. With a background in psychology and social work, topped with a certification in energy coaching, I've woven together scientific insights with personal experiences to offer you a multifaceted perspective on managing parenting challenges. This blend of personal transformation and professional expertise shapes this book's narrative and advice, making it a relatable and engaging journey for you.

As we progress, expect to explore various facets of emotional resilience, communication strategies, and real-life parenting scenarios. These scenarios are based on common parenting challenges, such as dealing with a child's tantrum or managing sibling conflicts. Each chapter builds on the last, creating a comprehensive map for your personal journey towards more mindful, effective parenting. Additionally, diverse parenting styles and challenges are discussed, ensuring that you will find value and understanding no matter your background or situation.

But this book is not just about information—it's about transformation. By the end of this journey, I hope you will not only grasp the importance of self-regulation in parenting but will also experience a profound shift in how you connect with your children and manage daily stresses. The potential for a more harmonious family life, with improved communication, reduced conflict, and increased emotional well-being, is not just a promise but an achievable outcome, and this book is your guide to unlocking that potential.

An optional workbook is available to unlock the power of self-reflection and action. Designed to complement your journey, it consolidates exercises from this current book that require thought and writing in one accessible place, fostering deeper understanding and facilitating practical application. The workbook includes guided reflections, practical exercises, and space for personal notes, all aimed at helping you apply the strategies discussed in the book to your own parenting experiences. By utilizing this workbook, you not only reinforce your learning but also pave the way for personal and family growth. Every revelation and realization finds a home within its pages, ensuring that the impact of your discoveries resonates long after you've turned the final page.

I invite you, with an open heart and mind, to engage deeply with the content of this book. Reflect on your parenting experiences, consider new perspectives, and be ready to transform how you interact within your family.

Let's close on a note of encouragement. Transformation is not just possible; it's within your reach. I believe in your ability to foster a nurturing, understanding, and resilient family environment. Together, let's step forward into a space where chaos becomes clear and parenting becomes an opportunity for personal growth and deep connection. Let this book be your guide and companion on that fulfilling journey.

Chapter One

The Foundation of Self-Regulation

Remember that morning when everything went wrong before 8 AM? The spilled coffee, the missing sock, the tantrum over the wrong pair of shoes—sometimes, it feels like the universe conspires to test your patience from the moment you open your eyes. In those moments, your response sets the tone for your day and, importantly, your child's day. Self-regulation in the context of parenting isn't just about maintaining order or discipline; it's fundamentally about managing your emotions and reactions under stress, setting a profound example for your children who are watching and learning from your every move.

1.1 Defining Self-Regulation in the Parenting Context

Self-regulation involves managing your emotions and maintaining control over your reactions in challenging situations. It's that deep breath you take before responding to your child's outburst or the calm demeanor you try to maintain when they test your limits. This concept might sound straightforward, but its implications in the parenting landscape are profound and far-reaching.

Why It Matters for Parents

Understanding and practicing self-regulation is crucial for creating a calm, nurturing environment at home. It's about more than just avoiding yelling or punishment; it's about demonstrating to your children how to handle their emotions in various situations. When you pause to compose yourself, you show your children that they, too, can pause and choose how to react to their feelings and frustrations. This environment is essential for their healthy emotional and psychological development. It gives them a sense of security and understanding, teaching them that it's okay to feel upset or angry and that these emotions can be managed constructively.

Impact on Family Dynamics

When you practice self-regulation, the benefits ripple across your family dynamics. It leads to more effective conflict resolution and strengthens the emotional connection between you and your children. Consider this: a home where parents can manage their stress and calmly respond to provocations has a foundation of peace and understanding. This stability is crucial for children as they navigate their own emotional development.

By handling your emotional responses, you minimize conflict and maximize understanding, creating an environment where your children feel safe to express themselves and confident in their value within the family. This secure base is not just about peace now; it lays the groundwork for your children's future relationships and emotional health.

Long-Term Benefits

The long-term benefits of self-regulation in parenting are profound. By managing your emotions effectively, you're teaching your children by example. Watching you teaches them to handle disappointments, manage stress, and negotiate conflicts. These skills are invaluable as they grow into adults who can navigate complex emotional landscapes in their own lives. Moreover, children raised in environments where emotions are managed healthily tend to perform better academically and socially because they spend less energy coping with emotional turbulence at home and more on learning and growing.

The Self-Regulation Cycle

To help visualize this concept, imagine self-regulation as a cycle:

1. **Trigger**: Something challenges your patience or emotional balance.

2. **Recognition**: You acknowledge your emotional response.

3. **Pause**: You take a moment to stop before reacting.

4. **Choose**: You decide the most constructive response.

5. **Act**: You respond in a way that aligns with your values and what you want to teach your child.

This cycle can be a quick mental checklist during stressful moments, providing a clear pathway from impulse to thoughtful action.

1.2 The Science Behind Self-Regulation: Bridging Biology and Behavior

Understanding the science behind self-regulation can significantly enlighten your parenting approach, especially when emotions run high. It's fascinating to see how much of our ability to regulate ourselves is deeply rooted in the brain's architecture, particularly in the prefrontal cortex. This area of the brain is like the conductor of an orchestra, overseeing decision-making, problem-solving, and regulating our impulses. When faced with the daily challenges of parenting—whether dealing with a teenager's mood swings or a toddler's tantrum—this part of your brain can help you decide how to respond calmly and effectively.

The prefrontal cortex fully develops in the mid-20s, which explains much about our children's sometimes impulsive and frustrating behavior. However, it also highlights a critical opportunity: the behaviors we model can influence the development of this part of their brains. Each time you take a deep breath instead of reacting, pause to choose your words carefully or make a conscious decision to approach a situation with empathy, you're not only regulating your own emotions but also teaching your children to do the same. This modeling directly impacts how their brains learn to handle stress and regulate emotions.

Moving deeper into the biological basis, our brains are wired to respond to stress in ways that once were protective but can now be challenging in modern parenting. When stress hits, whether it's from a screaming child or a near-miss car accident, our bodies flood with hormones like cortisol and adrenaline, preparing us for fight or flight. This response can be helpful in actual danger. Still, if we're constantly triggered by everyday parenting stress, it can lead to a cycle of reactive behavior. Understanding this can be a game changer. Recognizing that your heart racing or your palms sweating are just biological responses designed for a different era can give you that crucial moment to choose a different reaction. You might explain to your child, "Give me a moment; I'm feeling a bit overwhelmed," thereby modeling self-regulation in real time.

Additionally, the concept of emotional contagion plays a significant role in family dynamics. Have you ever noticed how a child's mood can drastically shift after they witness a parent in a bad mood? Emotions can spread like a cold in a household, for better or for worse. If you come home stressed and irritable, the rest of the family will likely tune into these emotions, leading to a domino effect of negativity. Conversely, if you manage to keep a positive, calm demeanor, you'll notice that it's easier for your children to remain stable as well. This isn't just about being in a good mood—it's about actively managing your emotional state to cultivate a more supportive and empathetic home environment.

Perhaps the most empowering aspect of brain science for parents is neuroplasticity. This term describes the brain's unique ability to reorganize itself by forming new neural connections throughout life. Neuroplasticity means that no matter how often you've found yourself losing your temper or feeling overwhelmed in the past, it's never too late to change those patterns. Each effort to regulate your responses strengthens new neural pathways, making calm, composed reactions more accessible over time. It's like forging a new path in a dense forest—the more you walk it, the clearer and easier to navigate it becomes. This change not only benefits you but also alters the emotional landscape of your entire family, setting a foundation for healthier, more resilient interactions.

By embracing these insights into how the brain and body interact, especially under stress, you can transform not just your parenting style but also the emotional health of your entire family. Understanding a bit of brain science can not only make you a more effective parent but also a more understanding one. Through consistent practice, guided by what we know of the brain, we can shift our family dynamics towards more positive, supportive, and loving interactions.

1.3 The Impact of Parental Emotions on Children

When we consider our influence on our children, direct interactions—discipline, support, teaching—often come to mind. However, it's equally, if not more, powerful to consider the indirect ways we shape our children, mainly through the emotional climate we create and model in our everyday lives. The emotions we express and how we manage them offer profound lessons to our children, impacting everything from their emotional intelligence to their sense of security and even their performance in school and social environments.

Modeling Behavior

Think about the last time you faced a stressful situation at home. Perhaps the dinner was burning, your phone was ringing, and your toddler chose that exact moment to test the limits of your patience. How you respond to such stressors—whether with calm problem-solving or with visible frustration—serves as a live demonstration to your children on handling emotions. This isn't just about maintaining peace at the moment but about instilling a method of managing life's inevitable challenges. In each instance where you model calmness and thoughtful response, you're teaching your child that these stressors are not catastrophes but manageable aspects of daily life. This modeling goes beyond mere behavior imitation; it ingrains in children a template for emotional regulation that they will carry into adulthood.

Furthermore, this consistent exposure to self-regulated behavior helps children develop a toolkit for emotional expression and control. They learn it's okay to feel overwhelmed but crucial to handle it constructively. This silent teaching forms the bedrock of their emotional intelligence, setting them up for success in adulthood.

Emotional Intelligence

The role of parental emotional regulation in nurturing a child's emotional intelligence cannot be overstated. Emotional intelligence, or EQ, involves more than recognizing one's own emotions; it also encompasses the management of these emotions, the ability to sense and understand others' feelings, and the skill to use this emotional awareness to guide thinking and behavior effectively. As parents, in every interaction where we display empathy, manage conflicts gracefully, and communicate our feelings clearly, we provide our children with critical lessons in emotional intelligence.

This development of EQ is crucial for children's social interactions and their understanding of complex emotional contexts. For instance, when a child observes their parent discussing a misunderstanding calmly with a partner or friend, they learn about perspective-taking and empathy. These skills are invaluable in building positive relationships both in childhood and later in life. Moreover, children with high EQ are better equipped to handle social nuances and resolve conflicts among peers, which are essential skills in the playground and the classroom.

Secure Attachment

A key aspect of emotional regulation's impact on children is its role in fostering secure attachment. Secure attachment forms when children feel consistently loved, understood and responded to by their parents. This security is foundational in developing trust, self-esteem, and resilience. When you, as a parent, respond to your child's needs and emotions predictively and sensitively—by acknowledging their feelings, providing comfort, and maintaining emotional availability even when you are stressed—you reinforce their sense of security.

This secure base then becomes a platform from which children explore the world, confident in the knowledge that they have a safe emotional haven to return to. It influences their approach to relationships and challenges, making them more willing to explore, take healthy risks, and innovate, knowing they have support if needed.

Academic and Social Success

Lastly, the influence of parental emotional regulation extends into the realms of academic and social success. Studies have shown that children who come from emotionally stable and responsive homes tend to perform better academically. This performance is not just a product of intellectual ability but also of emotional factors. For example, a child who has learned from their parents how to manage frustration and stay focused in the face of difficulty will be better equipped to handle the challenges of schoolwork. They are likelier to persist with complex tasks or confusing concepts because they've seen and internalized ways to regulate disappointment and confusion.

Socially, these children are often more adept at making friends and navigating social complexities. Their ability to empathize, learned from emotionally intelligent parents, makes them kinder and more considerate peers. Their experience in resolving conflicts at home provides them with strategies to manage disputes in school or play settings. Essentially, the emotional lessons taught at home echo through every area of a child's life, influencing not just who they are at home but who they become in the world.

Understanding the profound impact our emotional regulation has on our children highlights the responsibility and the opportunity we have as parents. Every moment of emotional interaction is a building block in your child's future, shaping their personality, abilities, and approach to life. By regulating our emotions, we do more than create a peaceful home; we equip our children with the tools they need to thrive emotionally, socially, and academically.

1.4 Self-Regulation vs. Self-Control: Understanding the Differences

In the bustling life of parenting, where every day feels like a new adventure filled with unexpected twists and turns, understanding the nuanced differences between self-regulation and self-control can be a game-changer. While these terms are often used interchangeably, they hold distinct meanings that can profoundly impact our approach to parenting. Self-regulation involves managing both your emotions and your responses to situations or stressors. It's about recognizing your feelings, understanding why you're experiencing them, and deciding how you'll respond in ways that align with your values and the parenting goals you've set. On the other hand, self-control is more about resisting immediate temptations and urges, such as not eating that last piece of cake or refraining from making an impulse purchase.

In the context of parenting, self-regulation reaches further and deeper than self-control. Consider a scenario where your child has just painted on the living room wall. Self-control might stop you from yelling immediately, but self-regulation involves understanding the frustration, acknowledging it, and then responding in a way that teaches your child about consequences and creativity without damaging their curiosity and confidence. This broader emotional and behavioral management framework makes self-regulation particularly crucial in parenting, where reactions are not just about maintaining order but about nurturing and guiding.

The implications of focusing on self-regulation rather than just self-control are significant, especially regarding discipline. Traditional discipline methods often lean heavily on self-control, emphasizing punishment and obedience without addressing the underlying emotions or the teachable moments that can arise from conflicts. A self-regulation approach, however, fosters a more empathetic environment. It encourages parents to look beyond the surface of the child's behavior to understand the emotions driving it. This understanding can lead to more effective and compassionate discipline strategies that teach children to manage their feelings and actions responsibly.

Imagine you're at the park, and your child throws a tantrum because it's time to leave. A self-control response might focus solely on suppressing your frustration and getting your child to go by any means necessary. A self-regulation response, however, would involve recognizing your irritation, calming yourself down, and then helping your child manage their disappointment, perhaps by acknowledging their feelings and discussing what you can do next time to make leaving easier. This not only helps in the moment but also builds your child's resilience over time.

In sum, while self-control is undoubtedly a valuable skill, it's self-regulation that offers the comprehensive emotional and behavioral management tools essential for effective parenting. By focusing on self-regulation, you not only manage your immediate reactions but also guide your children in developing the emotional intelligence and resilience they will need throughout their lives. This approach doesn't just make for smoother days; it builds a foundation of understanding, support, and emotional health that benefits the entire family.

Chapter Two

Identifying and Understanding Personal Triggers

I magine you're in the middle of cooking dinner, the kids are shouting in the living room, and suddenly, the pot boils over. Your heart races, your palms sweat, and you snap—over something seemingly small. Why does this happen? Often, it's not about the mess or the noise but something deeper, something triggered within you. This chapter is dedicated to unraveling these moments, understanding where they stem from, and how to handle them with grace and awareness.

2.1 Mapping Your Emotional Triggers: A Step-by-Step Guide

Identifying Triggers

The first step in mastering self-regulation is identifying what sets off your less-than-ideal responses. Triggers can be as varied as a child's whine, a partner's comment, or even a particular time of day. Recognizing these triggers is crucial because once you know what they are, you can begin to handle them constructively. Start by observing your reactions for a few days. Note what happens right before you feel upset or stressed. Is it a specific behavior from your child, a tone of voice, or perhaps a feeling of being overwhelmed? Keep a mental note or jot these down. You might start to notice patterns—certain situations or behaviors that consistently lead to discomfort or stress.

Understanding the Source

Now, delve into understanding why these triggers affect you. Often, our triggers are rooted in past experiences, unmet needs, or unresolved issues. For instance, if you find yourself particularly upset when your child does not listen to you, it could be linked to a deep-seated need for respect that stems from your own childhood experiences of feeling unheard. Understanding the source of your triggers is like detective work in your psychological landscape—it requires honesty and introspection but is crucial in helping you understand your reactions.

The Role of Self-Reflection

Self-reflection is a powerful tool in this journey. It involves stepping back, observing your emotions and reactions without judgment, and asking yourself, "Why did I react this way?" This practice can be challenging because it requires you to confront uncomfortable truths about yourself, but it is also incredibly freeing. By understanding the 'whys' behind your actions, you can begin to control your responses rather than letting your triggers control you.

Creating a Trigger Map

Once you've identified and understood your triggers, you can create a trigger map. This visual or written record lists common triggers and your typical reactions alongside more constructive responses you aim to adopt. For instance, if your child screams and you typically yell back, you might note a more constructive response, like taking three deep breaths before addressing them. This map will not only help you anticipate and prepare for potential stressors but will also serve as a reminder of the alternative responses you can choose to cultivate.

Create a simple chart with three columns. In the first column, list common triggers. In the second, note your usual reactions. In the third, outline more constructive responses. This chart serves as your personal guide in transforming reactionary impulses into thoughtful actions, helping to ease daily stress and improve interactions with your family.

By taking these steps—identifying triggers, understanding their origins, reflecting on your reactions, and mapping them out—you equip yourself with the knowledge and skills to handle challenging situations more effectively. This process enhances not only your well-being but also the emotional climate of your entire family, setting a positive example for your children and significantly improving your daily interactions.

2.2 From Trigger to Reaction: Breaking Down the Process

Understanding the mechanism of how triggers lead to reactions can be transformative. This sequence, often occurring in mere moments, typically flows from trigger to thought, then to emotion, and finally culminates in a reaction. Imagine this: you ask your child to turn off the TV and start their homework, but instead, they ignore you and continue watching. The trigger here is the child's non-compliance. Almost instantly, a thought flashes through your mind, perhaps something like, "They're ignoring me again!" This thought swiftly stirs up emotions—frustration and anger—which then fuel your reaction, possibly raising your voice or shutting off the TV abruptly.

Now, let's explore how we can interrupt this rapid sequence. The key lies in identifying the stages where intervention is most effective. Initially, becoming aware of the initial thought that follows the trigger offers a critical intervention point. By catching and examining this thought before it spirals into an emotional reaction, you can start to question its validity or explore other more constructive thoughts. For instance, considering whether the child didn't hear you or if they are engrossed in their program can shift your perspective and temper your emotional response.

At the emotional stage, techniques such as deep breathing or counting to ten can be very valuable. These methods help to decelerate the rush of emotions, providing a buffer time to evaluate the best response. This pause is crucial—it's where you have the power to choose your reaction rather than letting automatic responses dictate your actions. By consciously choosing how you react, for example, calmly turning off the TV and explaining the importance of homework time, you model self-regulation and problem-solving to your child.

Several parents have successfully implemented these strategies, transforming their family dynamics. Take Maria, a mother of two, who often found herself yelling when her children fought over toys. By understanding her trigger cycle, she started intervening at the thought stage. She reminded herself that children naturally test boundaries and that this was an opportunity to teach sharing and negotiation skills. With this new perspective, her emotional intensity decreased, and she could guide her children through conflict resolution calmly and effectively.

The power of choice in this process cannot be overstressed. Every step from trigger to reaction is a choice point—choosing to recognize the trigger, choosing to analyze the thought, choosing to manage the emotion, and finally, choosing the reaction. This empowerment through choice is what shifts parenting from reactive to proactive, from frustration to understanding, from chaos to harmony.

Using these insights and techniques allows you to transform not only how you respond to triggers but also how you view them. Instead of seeing a child's resistance to chores as a battle, it can be viewed as a teaching moment, an opportunity to foster independence and responsibility. This shift in perspective reduces stress and enhances the parenting experience, making daily interactions with your children more about connection and growth and less about conflict and frustration.

2.3 The Role of Past Experiences in Present Emotional Responses

Our past experiences, especially those from our own childhood, create a lens through which we view and interpret our children's actions. It's like walking through a house where the furniture is arranged according to an old blueprint. Sometimes, we bump into things because they're placed where they once were, not where we need them now. This is particularly true when unresolved issues from our past influence our reactions to our children's behavior. For example, if you grew up in a home where shouting was the norm during disagreements, you might find yourself raising your voice the moment any conflict arises, continuing a pattern laid down in your childhood. Understanding this connection between past and present can be a revelation, shedding light on why we react the way we do.

The impact of our childhood experiences on our current parenting style cannot be overstated. These formative years potentially set the stage for how we handle emotions, manage stress, and interact with our loved ones. If your emotional needs were consistently unmet as a child or if you were frequently criticized, you might find yourself overly sensitive to your child's comments or behavior that seem dismissive or judgmental. This sensitivity is not about the present moment, but a resonance of past hurts echoing in current interactions. There can also be patterns, experiences, and traumas from past relationships. Recognizing these patterns is the first step toward changing them. It involves a deep, sometimes uncomfortable introspection, but acknowledging these influences can empower you to choose different, healthier ways to relate to your children.

Breaking the cycle of past behaviors is crucial for fostering healthier family dynamics. This process starts with awareness but needs action to effect change. One effective strategy is actively choosing to respond differently from how your parents did or from the pattern you learned. This might mean, for example, taking a moment to breathe and consciously lowering your voice when you feel like shouting. It could involve using affirmations to bolster your patience and calm, reminding yourself that you are not your parents and you can choose a different path. Another powerful approach is creating new family rituals that promote positive interactions, such as regular family game nights or weekly dinners where each member shares something positive about their week. These activities build new, positive associations and memories, helping to overwrite the old patterns with new, healthier ones.

Consulting with therapists or counselors can be a transformative step in healing from past emotional traumas if you feel you need more guidance. These professionals offer valuable insights and practical techniques for addressing the wounds of your past, preventing their influence on your parenting. Therapy serves as a secure environment for dissecting past influences, adopting new coping mechanisms, and integrating these strategies into your parenting. Seeking assistance reflects strength, dedication to your family's health, and a commitment to personal development, ensuring your history enriches rather than dictates your and your children's futures.

In recognizing and addressing these past influences, you are not only working to improve your own emotional health but also actively protecting and nurturing your child's emotional development. This proactive approach helps ensure that your children will have a more positive blueprint to draw from when they become parents themselves, potentially benefiting generations to come. By breaking the cycle, you are setting a new standard, one that speaks of understanding, healing, and emotional resilience. This legacy of emotional health and conscious parenting is one of the most valuable gifts you can give to your children, far outweighing any material inheritance.

2.4 How Social Media and Comparisons Can Be an External Trigger

In today's digital age, social media has become a ubiquitous presence in our lives, offering both a window to the wider world and a mirror reflecting our personal lives. For parents, these platforms can inadvertently become a source of stress, particularly through the lens of comparison. Scrolling through feeds filled with seemingly perfect families, well-behaved children, and flawlessly organized homes can set an unattainable standard. This phenomenon, often referred to as the "comparison trap," can significantly undermine your self-regulation as a parent. It's easy to fall into the trap of measuring your everyday chaos against someone else's highlight reel, leading to feelings of inadequacy, frustration, and stress. These emotions can ripple through your interactions with your children and partner, potentially leading to impulsive reactions and strained relationships.

The impact of these comparisons is not just emotional but can also affect your parenting style. Confronted with images of "perfect parenting," you might find yourself pushing your children harder in academics or extracurricular activities, not out of a genuine understanding of their needs or interests, but to align with societal benchmarks showcased online. This pressure can create tension and conflict within the family, as children may resist these imposed expectations, leading to cycles of guilt and frustration that disrupt family harmony.

To counteract the negative effects of social media, setting healthy boundaries is crucial. Start by taking a proactive role in managing your online engagement. This might mean scheduling specific times for social media use rather than constant scrolling throughout the day. These scheduled periods can help you stay informed and connected without allowing social media to consume excessive amounts of your time and mental energy. Additionally, consider curating your social media feeds. Unfollow or mute accounts that trigger negative feelings of comparison or inadequacy and instead seek out pages that inspire, educate, and uplift. This selective approach can transform your social media experience from a source of stress to a supportive resource.

Moreover, it's beneficial to foster an environment of mindful consumption of social media. This practice involves being fully present and critically aware of how content influences your emotions and behaviors. Ask yourself questions like, "Why does this post trigger a sense of inadequacy?" or "What is it about this image that makes me feel anxious?" Understanding these reactions can help you develop healthier responses and detach your self-worth from online portrayals. Engaging with social media mindfully encourages you to consume content without letting it dictate how you feel about yourself and your parenting.

Another effective strategy is to use social media as a tool for connection rather than comparison. Focus on engaging with communities that share similar values and interests. Participate in groups that offer support and positive interactions. These platforms can be invaluable resources for advice, empathy, and encouragement, transforming social media into a supportive community that enhances your parenting journey rather than detracting from it.

In applying these strategies, you reclaim your power over how you interact with social media, ensuring that it serves as a positive influence in your life and not a source of triggers, stress or self-doubt. By setting boundaries, practicing mindful consumption, and fostering meaningful connections, you can enjoy the benefits of these platforms without falling into the comparison trap. This balanced approach to social media not only enhances your emotional well-being but also models healthy digital habits for your children, teaching them to use technology thoughtfully and responsibly.

2.5 Managing Expectations: Yours, Your Child's, and Society's

Have you ever found yourself staring down the barrel of a day that just didn't go as planned? Maybe the house was a mess despite your best efforts, the kids didn't quite behave as angels at the grocery store, or perhaps your meal didn't look anything like the Pinterest picture. It's easy to feel like you're falling short. Often, these feelings stem from the unrealistic expectations we set for ourselves, our children, and the ones we perceive from society. These expectations can be silent triggers, setting off a cascade of emotional responses when they're unmet.

In the whirlwind of parenting, where each day can bring new challenges, it's vital to step back and evaluate the expectations we carry. Are they really fair? Do they align with our family's values and reality, or are they borrowed standards from a glossy magazine or an over-idealized social media post? When we expect perfection—whether from ourselves or our children—we set the stage for disappointment. Perfection is an impossible standard, and striving for it can lead to frustration and a sense that we're not good enough.

This perfectionism pitfall is particularly dangerous in parenting. It can lead not only to personal stress and unhappiness but can also impact our children. They might feel constant pressure to meet these high standards, which can affect their self-esteem and happiness. It's important to shift our mindset from perfection to progress. Embracing a growth-oriented mindset helps us appreciate the small victories and incremental progress, both in ourselves and our children. It teaches kids that growth is more important than perfection and that making mistakes is a natural part of learning and developing.

Moreover, managing expectations isn't just about reducing them; it's about aligning them more closely with reality and our personal values. Start by having open conversations with your family about what's truly important. What values do you want to prioritize? Is it academic excellence, or is it kindness and creativity? By having these discussions, you can set goals and expectations that reflect what's genuinely important to your family rather than external societal standards.

Negotiating and adjusting these expectations is an ongoing process. It involves constant communication and the flexibility to shift perspectives when necessary. For instance, if you notice your child is overwhelmed by the schedule you thought was perfect, be ready to adjust it. Maybe they need more downtime or a different kind of support with their homework. Regular check-ins can help you stay tuned to your child's needs and adjust your expectations accordingly.

Also, it's helpful to practice setting realistic daily goals. Instead of aiming to have a spotless house, plan to organize just one area. Instead of hoping for a day without any tantrums or conflicts, prepare for how you'll constructively handle disagreements when they arise. This approach reduces the pressure on everyone in the family and helps inculcate a more relaxed, supportive environment.

Remember, the goal of managing expectations is not to lower standards or to stop striving for improvement but to create a more balanced, happy, and healthy family life where everyone can thrive. By being mindful of the expectations we set and adjusting them to be more in line with our true family values and reality, we foster a home environment where children feel valued for who they are, not just for their achievements or behavior. This nurturing atmosphere promotes confidence, resilience, and well-being, paving the way for children to grow into well-rounded and content individuals.

2.6 Journaling for Emotional Awareness and Trigger Tracking

The practice of journaling offers a unique blend of self-expression and self-discovery that can be particularly beneficial for parents navigating the emotional highs and lows of raising children. When you take the time to write down your thoughts and feelings, it's not just about offloading the day's stresses; it's about uncovering patterns in your emotional responses and triggers. This exercise can transform the way you understand yourself and interact with your family, offering clarity and calm in often chaotic parenting moments.

Benefits of Journaling

Writing regularly about your experiences and emotions can be incredibly therapeutic. It allows you to process emotions in a safe, private space where you're free to express everything from joy to frustration without fear of judgment. This process can be particularly enlightening when it comes to understanding what triggers certain responses in you. Over time, as you review your entries, you might begin to notice patterns—for instance, perhaps your stress peaks in the evenings when fatigue sets in, or maybe certain behaviors from your children trigger a stronger reaction because they remind you of past experiences. Recognizing these patterns is the first step toward managing them more effectively.

How to Start a Journal

If you're new to journaling, the idea of keeping a regular journal might seem daunting. However, it's easier to start than you might think. Choose a medium that feels comfortable, whether it's a traditional notebook, a digital app, or a simple document on your computer. Set a regular time each day to write, even if it's just five minutes before bed or while you have your morning coffee. Consistency is key. Write honestly and openly without worrying about grammar or style—the important thing is to capture your genuine thoughts and feelings. Over time, this practice will become a valuable part of your routine, offering insights and emotional release.

Reflective Questions

To deepen your journaling practice, consider using prompts that encourage you to reflect on your daily interactions and emotional responses. Here are a few to get you started:

- What moment today made me feel happiest, and why?

- Did I react today in a way I regret? What might I do differently next time?

- What am I grateful for today in my parenting journey?

- What triggered stress or anger in me today, and how did I handle it?

These questions can guide your writing and help you delve deeper into your emotional world, uncovering insights that might not be apparent in the rush of daily life. They prompt you to think critically about your reactions, decisions, and feelings, fostering greater self-awareness and emotional growth.

Reviewing and Learning

Regularly reviewing your journal entries allows you to track your progress, understand your setbacks, and recognize areas for growth. Set aside a time each week or month to read through your entries. This review can be eye-opening, as it allows you to see how far you've come and to identify ongoing challenges. It's also a chance to celebrate small victories—perhaps you handled a tough situation more calmly than before, or maybe you managed to turn a stressful moment into a teaching opportunity. These victories, big or small, are significant markers of your growth as a parent.

Optional Workbook: Practical Tools for Applying Concepts

A specially designed workbook is available to complement your journaling and the concepts discussed in this book. This resource is packed with exercises, additional journal prompts, and practical tools to help you apply the strategies we've explored. The purpose of this workbook is to offer a structured way to practice and deepen your understanding of self-regulation, emotional awareness, and effective parenting. It's a hands-on companion that encourages you to actively engage with the material, apply it in your daily life, and see tangible progress in your journey toward more mindful and responsive parenting.

By integrating journaling into your routine, you equip yourself with a power-ful tool for emotional regulation and self-discovery. This practice not only bene-fits you personally, offering stress relief and personal growth, but it also positively impacts your family dynamics. As you become more aware of your triggers and patterns, you can make more informed choices about how to respond to the challenges of parenting.

As we close this chapter, remember that each reflection, each moment of aware-ness, adds up, contributing to a more fulfilling and less reactive parenting experi-ence. As you continue to explore and grow through exercises and your journaling, you're setting the stage for more peaceful and positive family interactions, paving the way for a nurturing and supportive home life that benefits everyone.

Chapter Three

Strategies for Emotional Regulation

Navigating the journey of parenting can sometimes feel like sailing in stormy seas. Just as a skilled sailor uses tools to navigate rough waters, you can use emotional regulation strategies to steer through the day-to-day challenges of parenting. This chapter explores several essential techniques that help you stay calm in the moment and foster a serene atmosphere in your home, making the parenting voyage smoother for you and your children, empowering you to handle any situation with confidence and ease.

3.1 Breathing Techniques for Immediate Calm

The Science of Breathing

Let's dive into the science behind one of the most effective yet simple techniques for immediate calm: breathing. When you take deep, controlled breaths, you activate your body's parasympathetic nervous system—sometimes referred to as the "rest and digest" system. This activation counteracts the stress-induced responses initiated by the sympathetic nervous system, known for the "fight or flight" reaction. Deep breathing decreases heart rate and blood pressure, signaling to your body that it's time to calm down. This physiological change not only helps you feel calmer but also clears your mind, enhancing your ability to make thoughtful decisions in stressful parenting moments. The simplicity and effectiveness of this technique should reassure you that managing your stress and emotions is within your reach.

Practical Exercises

Let's go through some practical breathing exercises that you can use to regain your calm in those trying parenting moments. One effective technique is **box breathing**. Here's how you do it:

1. Inhale: Begin by inhaling slowly and deeply through your nose for a count of 4 seconds.

2. Hold: Once you've reached the full inhale, hold your breath for a count of 4 seconds.

3. Exhale: Slowly exhale through your mouth for another count of 4 seconds, emptying your lungs completely.

4. Hold: After exhaling, hold your breath again for 4 seconds before beginning the next cycle.

Do a few cycles or until you feel calmer. This technique is handy when you feel your stress levels rising, perhaps when homework time becomes a battleground or bedtime becomes a marathon. It helps induce relaxation, reduce stress, and promote a sense of calmness and focus.

Another simple yet powerful technique is **diaphragmatic breathing or belly breathing**. Here's how to practice it:

1. Sit comfortably, with one hand on your belly and the other on your chest.

2. Breathe in deeply through your nose, ensuring your belly pushes against your hand more than your chest does.

3. Breathe out through pursed lips as if you were whistling. Feel the hand on your belly go in, and use it to push all the air out.

4. Do this breathing 3 to 10 times. Take your time with each breath.

5. Notice how you feel at the end of the exercise.

Incorporating with Children

Breathing exercises aren't just for adults—children can significantly benefit from them too. Teaching your kids these techniques can help them manage their emotions, reducing tantrums and meltdowns. Make it a fun activity; perhaps imagine blowing up a balloon or feather across the table. This makes it engaging and helps them understand how to control their breathing.

Real-life Applications

Imagine it's one of those mornings where everything that can go wrong does. Your toddler spills juice on their clothes, your older child can't find their homework, and everyone is running late. Instead of letting the chaos lead to shouting or frustration, you can take a moment to practice box breathing. This pause and these breaths can shift the entire tone of the morning, helping you address each issue calmly and efficiently.

Incorporating Breathwork into Daily Routines

To make the most of breathwork, integrate it into your daily routine. Start your day with a minute of deep breathing before you even get out of bed. This sets a calm tone for the day ahead. You can also use breathing techniques during transitions, such as before leaving the car for school drop-off or before starting homework. This helps you and your children reset and prepare for the next activity with a clearer, calmer mindset.

Understanding the science behind it and regularly practicing these breathing techniques will equip you with a powerful tool to manage stress. This practice not only benefits you but also teaches your children practical ways to handle their own emotions, promoting a calmer, more harmonious family life.

3.2 The Power of Pause: Creating Space Between Stimulus and Response

In the midst of parenting's daily hustle, where quick reactions often become the norm, there's a powerful, transformative technique that can change not just moments but the very nature of your family interactions—pausing. This simple act of taking a brief halt before responding to children, partners, or any stressful situation allows you to shift from impulsive reactions to thoughtful responses. This pause is deeply rooted in the principle of mindfulness, which encourages a moment-by-moment awareness of our thoughts, emotions, and surroundings. By inserting a pause between a trigger (a child's tantrum, for instance) and your response, you give yourself space to breathe, assess, and then choose a reaction that aligns with your values and desired outcomes.

Practical Tips

Implementing the pause in everyday parenting can begin with some practical strategies. You might start by using verbal cues that become reminders to take this break. Phrases like "Let me think about this for a second" or "I need a moment to understand this better" help you stop and think and also demonstrate to your children how to handle frustration or confusion calmly. Physical reminders can also be effective. For instance, wearing a specific piece of jewelry or having a visible note in your living area or car that reads "Pause" can serve as a prompt to take that necessary breath before speaking or acting. A technique that can accompany you throughout your day is utilizing your phone. Set an alarm to go off at regular intervals with a simple reminder like "pause."

Another helpful strategy is to establish a 'pause protocol' during times of conflict or stress. This could be a family-agreed signal, like a timeout hand sign, that anyone can use to indicate the need to stop and take a breather, ensuring everyone respects this space without judgment. This teaches children that taking a moment to collect themselves is okay, fostering emotional regulation skills across your family.

Benefits for the Family

The benefits of adopting this pause are profound. It not only reduces conflict by lowering the chances of reacting in ways that escalate tensions but also sets a tone of respect and empathy within your household. By responding with more understanding and patience instead of snapping back in anger, you can increase mutual understanding and create a harmonious family environment. This can be particularly enlightening when dealing with children who may not consistently articulate their emotions clearly, leading to more joyful and fulfilling family interactions.

This technique doesn't just prevent negative outcomes—it significantly enriches your family life. It teaches children crucial emotional management and problem-solving skills, fostering an environment of mutual respect and understanding. It also turns challenging moments into opportunities for growth and connection within the family.

Parenting Challenges

Consider a common scenario: your teenager has forgotten to do their chores again, and your initial impulse might be frustration or disappointment. Here, the power of pause allows you to approach the situation differently. Instead of a possibly heated exchange, pausing helps you consider why they might have forgotten. You can then address the issue from a place of wanting to understand, perhaps uncovering underlying reasons like stress from schoolwork or a simple misunderstanding of expectations. This approach solves the immediate issue more effectively and strengthens your communication and relationship.

Another example could be dealing with a young child's meltdown. It's easy to react quickly with a reprimand when you're in a public place and feeling the eyes of judgment, but pausing helps you respond in a way that meets your child's needs rather than just soothing societal pressures. It allows you to kneel down, acknowledge their frustration, and guide them through their feelings, which teaches them emotional regulation through your example.

Incorporating the power of pause into your parenting toolkit transforms your family's dynamics. It changes how conflicts are resolved, how emotions are handled, and how your family interacts daily. This simple act of pausing ensures that you aren't just reacting to the waves of daily challenges but thoughtfully navigating through them, creating a calmer, more understanding family environment. It's a gift of space and time that benefits everyone, making each day a little smoother and each challenge a little more manageable.

3.3 Using Physical Space to Regain Emotional Balance

The environment around us can profoundly influence our emotional state, often more than we realize. When you're overwhelmed or stressed, changing your surroundings can be as effective as any deep breathing exercise or meditation technique. It's about more than mere aesthetics; it's about creating spaces that actively contribute to your calm. This transformation can be particularly powerful in a home setting, where the line between chaos and calm can be thin, especially with children.

The Role of Environment in Emotional Regulation

Consider how different environments affect your mood. A cluttered, chaotic room might amplify feelings of stress and frustration. In contrast, a clean, organized space can promote a sense of calm and control. This isn't just an individual preference but a widely recognized psychological response. Studies have shown that physical clutter in your surroundings competes for your attention, resulting in decreased performance and increased stress. These findings underline the importance of creating a physical environment that can help, rather than hinder, your emotional regulation efforts. By consciously shaping the spaces where you spend most of your time, you can foster an atmosphere that reduces stress and enhances your ability to manage it when it arises.

Creating a Calm Space

One effective way to use your environment to support emotional well-being is to establish a designated calm space in your home. This doesn't need to be an entire room; even a tiny, specific corner can serve as a retreat from the hustle and bustle of family life. This space should be tailored to induce calmness, filled with elements that soothe you—scented candles, soft pillows, calming colors, or photos of cherished memories. The key is to create an area that feels like a sanctuary where you can step away for a few minutes to gather your thoughts and emotions.

Encourage every family member to create their own calm space. For children, this could be a corner of their room with comfy bean bags, their favorite books, and soft lighting. Encouraging children to participate in designing their space not only makes it more likely they will use it but also teaches them about managing their emotions through their environment.

Using Nature as a Reset

Beyond the confines of your home, nature offers its own powerful brand of emotional recalibration. The benefits of spending time in natural surroundings are well-documented, with studies showing that it can lower blood pressure, reduce stress hormone levels, and enhance feelings of well-being. Whether it's a backyard, a local park, or just a tree-lined street, spending time in nature can be a significant mood booster.

Make it a routine to incorporate nature into your family's life. It could be as simple as walking the dog together after dinner or spending part of the weekend at a local park. These moments provide a break from indoor constraints and screen time and allow you and your children to connect with the calming effects of the natural world. This connection to nature can act as a grounding force, reminding you and your family of the world outside your immediate concerns and stresses, providing a broader perspective that can be soothing.

Physical Space and Mindful Awareness

Linking physical space with mindfulness enhances the emotional benefits of both. Mindful awareness—paying attention to the present moment without judgment—can transform how you interact with your environment. It involves not just being in a space but really noticing and appreciating aspects of it: the way light filters through a window, the textures of the furniture, and the sounds that float in from outside. This practice can turn ordinary spaces into rich sensory experiences that draw your attention away from stressors and refocus on the here and now.

To integrate this approach into your daily life, start by making small changes to your routine. For instance, if you work from home, take a few moments before you start your day to sit in your designated work space and consciously observe the setting. Note the items that make you feel at ease and those that don't. Maybe a stack of unsorted papers is causing a subtle tension; dealing with it could help you start your day with a clearer mind.

Similarly, encourage your children to engage mindfully with their spaces. Before bedtime, you might have a short routine where your child tidies their calm corner and talks about what each item means to them. This helps them care for their space and teaches them to use their surroundings to manage their feelings, a skill that will serve them well beyond the walls of your home.

By actively using and adapting your physical environments, you create external conditions that support internal calm and balance. This proactive approach to emotional regulation not only enhances your well-being but also sets a powerful example for your children about the importance of caring for their surroundings and, by extension, for themselves.

3.4 The Art of Positive Self-Talk in Stressful Moments

The words we speak to ourselves in times of stress or challenge wield immense power, influencing our emotions and actions. This internal dialogue can either escalate our stress (making us feel overwhelmed and incapable) or soothe and empower us (reminding us of our strengths and abilities). Understanding the power of language in our internal conversations is crucial, especially for parents who are often in the eye of the storm, managing both their emotions and those of their children. When we talk to ourselves with criticism or doubt, it's like adding fuel to an already blazing fire. It intensifies our stress and can make us react in ways we later regret. Conversely, when we consciously shift our internal speech to be more positive and supportive, it's like pouring water on the flames, calming our minds and allowing us to handle situations with more clarity and patience.

Techniques for Positive Self-Talk

To harness the calming power of positive self-talk, consider incorporating specific phrases or mantras into your daily routine, especially before situations that typically stress you out. Phrases like "I can handle this," "This moment is tough, but so am I," or "I am doing my best, and that's enough" can be powerful tools. These simple affirmations can help shift your mindset from inadequacy or frustration to strength and resilience. Here's how you can start:

1. Identify stress points in your day, perhaps morning rush hours or bed-time routines.

2. Create a few short, positive affirmations relevant to these moments.

3. Repeat these affirmations to yourself during these times or whenever you feel stress rising. This practice might feel forced at first, but over time, these positive affirmations become part of your automatic thoughts, naturally kicking in when stress levels rise.

Rewriting the Narrative

Changing habitual negative thought patterns into positive narratives is a transformative process that involves awareness, practice, and persistence. Begin by simply noticing your negative self-talk. Each time a harsh or critical thought crosses your mind, acknowledge it without judgment and then actively reframe it into something positive. For example, if you catch yourself thinking, "I'm a bad parent," pause and reframe it to, "I'm a parent who makes mistakes like everyone else, and I'm continually learning and growing." This method of cognitive restructuring, a term psychologists use for changing thought patterns, helps break down old, negative thinking habits and build new, more positive ones in their place. It's like rewiring your brain to focus on your strengths and efforts rather than your perceived failures.

The Ripple Effect on Children

The benefits of positive self-talk extend beyond your own emotional health. This practice also sets a powerful example for your children. They learn to mimic this approach when they see you managing stress and setbacks with positive self-talk. Imagine dropping a pebble into a pond; the ripples created by this small act spread far and wide. Similarly, when you model positive self-talk, your children learn to be kinder and more compassionate with themselves. This modeling can profoundly impact their self-esteem and emotional resilience. Additionally, this practice can help create a more positive home environment where encouragement and support replace criticism and doubt, benefiting everyone's mental and emotional well-being.

By embracing the power of positive self-talk, you transform your ability to manage stress and challenges and the foundation of family interactions, promoting a healthier, more nurturing home life for everyone involved.

3.5 Cultivating Patience: Long-Term Strategies for Emotional Resilience

Patience is often painted with a broad brush as merely the ability to wait calmly, whether in line at the grocery store or for your toddler to finally put on their shoes by themselves. But patience in the context of parenting also means handling stress, managing expectations, and persisting through challenges without immediate rewards. Understanding and cultivating this kind of patience can significantly enhance your emotional resilience, transforming how you interact with your children and respond to family life's inevitable ups and downs.

Building patience is not about suppressing your emotions or ignoring your needs; instead, it's about developing a deeper understanding of your emotional triggers and learning to respond to them in a balanced and thoughtful way. One effective strategy is to set small, achievable goals that lead to larger objectives. For instance, if evening routines with your children are typically stressful, start with the goal of having just one evening a week, where you focus on making the process more enjoyable and less rushed. This could involve preparing parts of dinner ahead of time or setting out clothes the night before. Celebrating these small wins can boost your sense of efficacy and encourage you to keep building on these positive changes, gradually increasing your patience and reducing evening stress.

Practicing gratitude is another powerful tool in this endeavor. By consciously acknowledging the aspects of parenting and of your children that you're grateful for, you can shift your focus from frustrations to appreciation. This shift doesn't negate the challenges but puts them in a broader, more balanced perspective that makes them easier to handle. Each night, you might reflect on a moment with your children that made you smile or feel connected. This practice not only reinforces your patience but also deepens your relationship with your children by highlighting the positive interactions that might otherwise be overshadowed by day-to-day stresses.

Modeling patience for your children is perhaps one of the most impactful aspects of cultivating this trait. Children learn how to handle frustration and delay gratification primarily by observing how their parents manage these challenges. When they see you handling a stressful situation with calm and composure, they learn that these reactions are not only possible but preferable. You can explicitly teach patience through activities that require waiting, such as baking, where they can see that waiting for the cookies to bake results in a delicious reward. Discuss with them how impatience is normal, but we can focus on other things or use the time productively while waiting.

The stories of transformation that emerge from parents who have worked to develop their patience are both inspiring and instructive. Take, for instance, a father named Lucas, who struggled with impatience when his children were slow to complete tasks. He focused on building his patience by setting small goals for himself, such as waiting a few extra minutes before intervening when his children dressed themselves or did their chores. Over time, his children became more proficient at these tasks, and the morning routine became less fraught. Lucas found that as his patience increased, so did his enjoyment of fatherhood. His children also became more confident and independent, knowing they had the time and space to tackle tasks on their own. This story underscores how patience not only improves the immediate family environment but also fosters long-term emotional resilience and independence in children.

By understanding the more profound value of patience in parenting, implementing practical strategies to cultivate it, and modeling it for your children, you can enhance your family's emotional environment and your own emotional resilience. It becomes a vital component of a healthy, happy family life, enriching your relationships and teaching your children valuable emotional skills that will serve them throughout their lives.

3.6 The Role of Physical Exercise in Enhancing Emotional Stability

The connection between physical activity and emotional well-being is well-documented yet often underestimated, especially in the context of parenting. Regular exercise can significantly bolster your emotional resilience, providing a natural and effective outlet for stress relief. Studies have shown that physical activity stimulates the production of endorphins, the body's natural mood lifters. This biochemical process is crucial for parents who often navigate high-stress environments, balancing the demands of family life with personal and professional responsibilities.

Exercise also impacts our emotional health by improving our sleep quality and reducing levels of anxiety and depression, making us more equipped to handle the emotional challenges of parenting. For example, a brisk walk or a bike ride after a stressful day can help clear your mind and lower your stress levels, making you more present and patient when interacting with your children. Moreover, regular physical activity helps maintain healthy brain function, which includes enhanced cognitive abilities, better memory, and sharper decision-making skills—assets that every parent can benefit from.

Integrating exercise into your family life can also be a fantastic way to foster emotional regulation skills in your children. Participating in family fitness activities sets a healthy example and provides a fun and engaging way to release pent-up energy, which can be particularly beneficial for children. These activities can range from family yoga sessions, which can be calming and centering, to more vigorous activities like hiking or cycling, which are great for burning energy and improving overall fitness.

To make these activities a regular part of your family routine, schedule them just as you would any important appointment. Every Saturday morning could be your family hike day, or maybe Wednesday evenings could be reserved for biking through your local park. The key is consistency and commitment, as the regularity of these activities reinforces their importance, not just for physical health but also for emotional well-being.

Addressing common barriers to regular exercise is crucial, especially for busy parents. Time constraints are often the biggest challenge, but this can be managed by integrating physical activity into your daily routines. For instance, consider walking or biking instead of driving your kids to school if it's a realistic option. Not only does this provide an excellent start to the day for both you and your kids, but it also incorporates exercise seamlessly into your daily life. Another common barrier is a lack of motivation, which can be countered by setting small, achievable fitness goals that provide a sense of accomplishment. Additionally, involving the entire family can create a supportive environment that encourages everyone to stay active.

By providing practical ways to integrate activity into daily life, you can enhance not only your own emotional resilience but also model healthy behaviors for your children. This proactive approach to fitness encourages a lifestyle that values and prioritizes well-being, making it easier to manage the psychological demands of parenting while fostering a joyful and active family environment.

3.7 Overcoming Resistance to Change

Change, especially as a parent, often feels like turning a ship on high seas. It's slow and requires effort, and sometimes, you'd rather maintain the current course than face the turbulent waters of transformation. But understanding why we resist change can be a game-changer in itself, helping to unlock growth in ourselves and within our whole family dynamic.

Resistance to change often stems from fear—fear of the unknown, fear of failure, or even fear of success. These fears can keep us locked in comfortable patterns, even when they're not serving us well. Think of it like holding onto an old, heavy suitcase because we can't see what's ahead on the journey; dropping it feels risky, even if it makes the walk harder. Psychologically, this resistance is often rooted in a natural human preference for predictability and control. Introducing change, whether it's shifting a parenting strategy or altering a daily routine, disrupts this predictability.

Acknowledging this resistance is the first step towards overcoming it. Self-awareness plays a pivotal role here—it's about understanding your emotional responses to change and recognizing the triggers that make you cling to the status quo. This might involve reflecting on moments when you felt a change was necessary but hesitated or pulled back at the last moment. By identifying these patterns, you can start to address them more constructively.

One practical strategy to overcome resistance is to start small. Big changes can be overwhelming, increasing the likelihood of resistance. Instead, break down the change into manageable, less intimidating steps. For instance, to incorporate more patience into your parenting, start by focusing on one specific part of the day, like dinner time. Commit to approaching this time with a new perspective for one week and observe the effects. Small successes can build confidence and decrease resistance, making larger changes feel more achievable.

Embracing discomfort is another crucial strategy. Change is inherently uncomfortable; it pushes you out of your comfort zone and challenges your norms. However, viewing this discomfort as a growth opportunity can transform your experience of it. When you feel uneasy about a new parenting method or a routine change, remember that growth often feels uncomfortable at first. This discomfort isn't a sign that something is wrong but rather that something is shifting. It's a sign of potential growth and development, not just for you but for your family, too.

By understanding the roots of resistance, leveraging self-awareness to address it, and adopting practical strategies to manage the discomfort it brings, you can start to see change not as a threat but as an opportunity. This shift in perspective can significantly enhance your ability to grow as a parent and lead your family through changes that improve your collective well-being and happiness.

As this chapter closes, reflect on the strategies discussed and consider how they can be applied to your parenting journey. When incorporated mindfully and consistently, these practices can empower you to navigate challenging situations with composure and empathy. Next, we'll explore approaches to nurturing effective communication channels between parents and children, unlocking the potential for deeper connections and mutual understanding.

Chapter Four

Communication that Connects

I magine you're at a bustling family reunion, where conversations flow like a lively stream, full of laughter and overlapping voices. Now, picture a moment within that scene—a child tugging at your sleeve, trying to tell you about their newly drawn masterpiece. At the same time, you nod absentmindedly, half-listening, half-lost in the adult banter. In these split-focus scenarios, the essence of connection can slip through our fingers, leaving both child and parent feeling unheard and undervalued. This chapter dives into the heart of effective communication. It's not just about hearing the words; it's about understanding the emotions and meanings behind them and building a bridge of empathy and trust between you and your child.

4.1 Active Listening: The First Step to Understanding Your Child

Principles of Active Listening

Active listening is foundational to effective communication and connection because it involves fully concentrating, understanding, responding, and remembering what is being said. This kind of listening is active because you engage with the speaker both verbally and non-verbally, showing that you are not merely hearing their words but also processing and responding to them thoughtfully. The power of this engagement lies in its simplicity and its challenge—it requires us to put aside our own thoughts and judgments momentarily to truly tune into another human being's emotional or verbal expression.

Active Listening Techniques

Practicing active listening is more manageable than it may seem. Start with your body language: orient your body toward your child, make eye contact, and nod to show you're engaged. These non-verbal cues communicate that you are present and focused on the conversation. Verbal affirmations like 'I see,' 'Tell me more about that,' or 'That sounds important' also play a crucial role. They encourage your child to continue and show that you value what they're expressing. Another key technique is reflective responses, which involve paraphrasing or summarizing your child's words. This not only shows that you are listening but also helps clarify and confirm your understanding of their message.

The Impact of Validating Feelings

Acknowledging and validating a child's feelings is a powerful aspect of active listening. When you validate your child's emotions, you communicate that their feelings are important and legitimate, which can significantly strengthen your bond. Validation can be as simple as saying, "It sounds like you're really excited about this," or "I can understand why that upset you." This kind of empathetic response helps children feel supported and loved, fostering a deeper connection and trust between you and your child.

Overcoming Listening Barriers

Common barriers to active listening, especially in parent-child interactions, include distractions, preconceived notions, and emotional reactions. Overcoming these barriers often requires intentional effort. Minimize distractions by setting aside specific times for one-on-one conversations with your child when you can give them your full attention. Work on recognizing and setting aside your biases or preconceived notions about what your child is saying; this allows you to listen with an open mind. Additionally, manage your emotional reactions by reminding yourself that the goal of the conversation is to understand and connect with your child, not to judge or lecture.

> **Acronym to help you remember essential elements**
> - **L**ook at your child
>
> - **I**nvite them to share (e.g., "Would you like to tell me more about what happened today?")
>
> - **S**ummarize what they say (e.g., "So, you're upset because you didn't get to play the game you wanted.")
>
> - **T**hank them for sharing
>
> - **E**ncourage with open-ended questions (e.g., "How did that make you feel?" or "What do you think about that?")
>
> - **N**od and use **N**on-verbal cues (e.g., Nod your head, smile, and use expressions like "I see" to show you're engaged.)

Active Listening in Practice

Consider the power of active listening in a challenging conversation. When a child is upset about a bad day at school, instead of offering immediate advice or solutions, a parent practicing active listening might say, 'It sounds like you had a really tough day. Want to tell me more about what happened?' This approach allows the child to explore their feelings and thoughts, often leading to a more open and resolving dialogue. It shifts the dynamic from one of problem-solving to empathy and understanding, which can profoundly impact the child's ability to cope with and overcome their challenges.

Active listening is not just a communication technique; it's a transformative tool that can enrich your relationship with your child. It's a gift of presence that tells them that we value their thoughts and feelings and are here to support and understand them, not just to direct or correct them. This chapter aims to equip you with the tools you need to harness the power of active listening, transforming everyday conversations into moments of genuine connection and mutual respect. As you practice these skills, you'll likely discover not just a deeper connection with your child but also insights into their thoughts, feelings, and worldviews that can enrich your relationship in ways you never anticipated.

4.2 Speaking So Your Child Will Listen: Techniques for Every Age

When we talk about communicating with our children, it's not just about the words we use but how we convey them. Tailoring our language to be age-appropriate is crucial, as what works for a teenager won't necessarily resonate with a toddler. For the youngest of our kids, simple, concrete language cuts through the fog of their burgeoning understanding of the world. When you ask a toddler to clean up their toys, instead of saying, "Can you organize your toys?" a more explicit directive like "Please put your blocks in the box and your dolls on the shelf" breaks down the task into manageable steps that align with their cognitive abilities. As children grow, their comprehension deepens, and their capacity for abstract thinking matures. This development allows for more complex conversations that involve reasoning and the discussion of consequences. For teenagers, for instance, conversations about curfews might include the reasoning behind them, such as safety concerns, rather than a simple directive to be home by a specific time.

In fostering cooperative behavior and open communication, the role of positive reinforcement cannot be understated. Children, much like adults, respond well to encouragement and acknowledgment of their efforts. Praising your child not only for achievements but also for their effort fosters an environment where they feel valued and motivated to engage. This positive reinforcement strengthens your communication channels. When children believe their actions are noticed and appreciated, they are more likely to listen and cooperate. For example, instead of only acknowledging your child's clean room, praise the effort it took, especially if they maintained it clean for a whole week. Say something like, "I really appreciate how you've kept your room tidy all week; I know it takes a lot of effort to keep it looking so nice."

However, it's about more than what we encourage; it is also about how we guide. As parents, there's often a temptation to lecture, especially when our children are not listening or following directions. Yet, lectures can make children feel like they're being talked at rather than talked to, often leading to tuning out or defiance. An alternative to lecturing is storytelling, where moral lessons or guidance are woven into stories that engage a child's imagination and emotions. For a young child, a story about a little bear who cleaned up his toys to make room for a fun new game can be more effective than a lecture about cleanliness. For older children, discussing the consequences of actions in a narrative about someone they can relate to can lead to deeper understanding and self-reflection.

Keeping messages clear and concise is another cornerstone of effective communication. Children have varying attention spans, often influenced by their age, and a message lost in a sea of words is a message not heard. Be direct but kind, ensuring your child understands what is being asked without feeling overwhelmed by information. For instance, if you need your child to do their homework, instead of a vague "do your homework before bed," a more effective directive would be, "Please start your homework at 5 PM so you have plenty of time before dinner." This not only sets a clear expectation but also a timeframe that helps your child understand exactly what is required and when.

- Tailor language to age: Adjust communication for different developmental stages, using simple language for young children and more complex reasoning for teenagers.

- Utilize positive reinforcement: Encourage and acknowledge effort, not just achievements, to foster motivation and cooperation.

- Avoid lecturing: Instead of lecturing, engage children through storytelling to convey guidance effectively.

- Keep messages clear and concise: Provide direct and understandable instructions, considering children's varying attention spans.

By adjusting our communication techniques to fit our child's age, providing positive reinforcement to encourage good behaviors, substituting lectures with engaging alternatives, and ensuring our messages are clear and concise, we lay the groundwork for not just being heard but truly listened to. These strategies foster an atmosphere of respect and openness, making our children feel secure and understood and more likely to engage positively with us and the world around them.

4.3 Navigating Difficult Conversations with Your Child with Grace

When the time comes to sit down with your child and discuss something challenging—whether it's about poor grades, a misunderstanding with friends, or changes in the family dynamics such as a move or divorce—how you prepare for and manage the conversation can significantly influence the outcome. The art of handling these delicate discussions gracefully is something every parent can master with thoughtful preparation and empathy.

Preparing for Difficult Conversations

The key to preparing for a difficult conversation is considering timing and setting, which can profoundly impact how the message is received. Choose a time when both you and your child are calm and not rushed. This might mean waiting until after dinner when the day's pressures have eased, rather than right after school when your child may still be processing their day. The setting should be private and comfortable, a place where your child feels safe to express themselves without fear of being overheard or interrupted. It could be their favorite corner in the living room with cozy chairs or a quiet walk in the park. Before you start the conversation, it helps to plan out the main points you want to address. This doesn't mean scripting everything you'll say but having a clear understanding of the topics you need to cover and the feelings you want to convey. This preparation can help you stay focused and make the conversation more constructive.

Communicating with Sensitivity

When discussing sensitive topics, your language and tone are as important as the words themselves. Speak with clarity and simplicity, making sure your language is age-appropriate. Regardless of age, all children benefit from a gentle tone and a pace that allows them to digest the information being shared. Most importantly, empathy must drive the conversation. Try to see the situation from your child's perspective and acknowledge their feelings as valid. Statements like, "I can see why you might feel that way," or "It's okay to feel upset about this" help validate their emotions, making them more open to dialogue.

Managing Emotions

Managing your emotions is one of the toughest parts of navigating difficult conversations. It's natural to feel anxious, upset, or even angry, depending on the topic. However, maintaining your composure is crucial to ensure the conversation remains constructive. Techniques such as deep breathing before and during the discussion can help keep your emotions in check. Also, if the conversation gets too heated or emotional, it's perfectly okay to take a break and revisit the discussion later. I invite you to try different techniques from this book, such as changing your environment. This can prevent the conversation from escalating into a conflict and demonstrates to your child that taking time to process emotions effectively is important.

Examples of Difficult Conversations

Consider a scenario where you must talk to your child about why they've been avoiding school. Instead of directly confronting them, you could start by expressing your observations and concerns, "I've noticed you seem unhappy about going to school lately, and I'm worried because I know how much you usually love your classes." This opens up a space for them to share, with your observation acting as an invitation to discuss their feelings. Another example could be discussing a family issue like a financial setback that requires cutting back on expenses. Explaining the situation honestly while ensuring their security helps manage expectations and emotions, "Things are a bit tight right now, and we might need to skip our summer vacation. But we're all together and will find fun ways to make this summer special at home."

Success in these conversations often comes from a blend of honest expression, empathetic listening, and mutual respect for each other's feelings. By approaching these discussions with preparation, sensitivity, and calm, you foster an environment where difficult topics can be navigated with trust and openness, reinforcing your relationship and providing your child with the tools to handle challenging situations constructively in the future.

4.4 Conflict Resolution

Empathy serves as the foundation for resolving conflicts with your child. When a disagreement arises, instead of immediately asserting authority, try to understand your child's perspective. Ask them to explain their thoughts and feelings about the situation. This shows respect for their viewpoint and helps you understand the motivation behind their behavior. From here, you can guide them towards a resolution that considers both your perspectives. This empathetic approach resolves the immediate conflict and strengthens your relationship by building mutual respect and understanding.

4.5 The Power of Apology: Teaching by Example

In the fabric of family life, mistakes are as inevitable as the laundry that piles up by the end of the week. As parents, we navigate a constant learning curve, and yes, this means occasionally slipping up. The art of apologizing to our children when we err is not just about saying "I'm sorry" but about turning these moments into profound teaching opportunities. When we apologize to our children, we do more than rectify a wrong. We are teaching them about accountability, the value of integrity, and the strength to admit mistakes.

Apologizing effectively to your child involves several key steps that ensure the apology not only addresses the mistake but also aids in healing any emotional rifts it may have caused. First, a genuine apology begins with the acknowledgment of the wrongdoing. Be specific about what you are apologizing for. This clarity shows that you understand the impact of your actions. For example, instead of a vague "I'm sorry for earlier," opt for, "I'm sorry I raised my voice when you asked for help with your homework. You needed support, and I responded with frustration." This detailed acknowledgment helps your child understand what the apology is for and validates their feelings regarding the incident.

Next, express sincere regret for your actions and their impact on your child. This step is crucial as it communicates your empathy for how your actions affected their feelings. It's about showing that you care that your child felt hurt or upset by your actions. You might say, "I regret that I spoke harshly—it wasn't fair to you, and I can see how it upset you." This expression of regret helps to reinforce the emotional bond between you and your child, showing them that their feelings matter to you.

Furthermore, a commitment to change is essential to an effective apology. This means expressing your intention to handle similar situations differently in the future. It could be as straightforward as, "Next time, I'll take a moment to breathe and listen fully before I respond." This promise helps to rebuild trust and sets a positive example for your children about handling personal mistakes and growth.

The impact of such apologies on children can be significant. When children see their parents apologize, they learn that everyone, regardless of age or role, is responsible for making amends when they do wrong. This understanding fosters a sense of fairness and justice. Moreover, by witnessing their parents handle mistakes with integrity, children learn the importance of empathy and forgiveness. They see firsthand how acknowledging one's faults and addressing them can mend and even strengthen relationships, which are invaluable lessons for their future social interactions.

To practice this in your family, consider having regular family meetings where each member, including parents, can express if something upset them and discuss resolutions openly. During these sessions, practice apologizing where necessary. These meetings can become a safe space for all family members to air grievances and resolve them constructively, reinforcing the practice and importance of sincere apologies and effective communication.

In weaving the thread of sincere apologies into the tapestry of daily family life, you not only correct your missteps but also enrich the relational dynamics within your family. This practice of openly acknowledging mistakes and working through them together fosters an environment of trust, respect, and mutual growth. As your family learns to navigate apologies and forgiveness, you build a stronger, more connected unit equipped to handle whatever challenges come your way with grace and understanding.

Let's remember the lessons woven through our discussions in this chapter: the transformative power of active listening, the art of speaking so children will listen, gracefully navigating difficult conversations and conflicts, and the power of apology. Each of these elements prepares us to engage deeply, respond thoughtfully, and guide lovingly. As we turn the page, we will explore how these foundational communication skills extend beyond words into the actions and daily rhythms that shape our family lives.

Chapter Five

Establishing a Positive Family Dynamic

I magine the close of a challenging day, and your home is alive with your children's laughter and lively conversations. Amid this everyday chaos, you notice your youngest child drawing on the living room walls with markers, challenging the limits of your newly painted surfaces. It's natural to want to respond with a firm "No!" However, consider the possibility of approaching this scenario differently. What if this situation could be transformed into an invaluable lesson on setting boundaries, demonstrating respect, and caring for personal and shared spaces? This chapter explores the fundamental role of establishing boundaries and different elements for a peaceful and cohesive family environment.

5.1 Setting Boundaries with Love: The Foundation of a Harmonious Home

Importance of Boundaries

Boundaries in a family are essential for creating an environment where every member, from the youngest to the oldest, understands their rights and responsibilities. They help in defining what is acceptable and what is not, which, in turn, fosters a sense of security and stability. Children thrive in environments where they know what to expect. When boundaries are clear, children feel safe to explore, learn, and eventually understand their limits and those of others. This understanding is crucial not only for their immediate behavior but also for their lifelong interpersonal skills.

Strategies for Setting Boundaries

Setting boundaries effectively starts with clear communication. It's about being explicit about your expectations in an understandable way for your child. For instance, rather than saying "be good," specify what "being good" looks like in that context. Is it using indoor voices, sharing toys, or asking for things politely? Be clear, and involve your children in the conversation about why these boundaries exist. Let them ask questions and express their feelings about these rules. This inclusion helps them feel respected and part of the family decision-making process.

Consistency is another pillar in effective boundary-setting. Consistency in enforcing rules removes confusion, helping children internalize what they are expected to do. However, life isn't always black and white, and there might be times when flexibility is necessary. In such cases, explain why exceptions are made, ensuring that these exceptions don't become the rule.

Open communication channels are vital. They ensure that setting boundaries is a two-way street. Encourage your children to express how they feel about certain rules. Sometimes, listening to their perspective might lead to adjustments that better suit the family's changing dynamics. For example, bedtime might need adjustment as children grow older and their school demands change.

Balancing Firmness and Compassion

Balancing firmness and compassion might be one of the trickiest aspects of parenting. It's about enforcing rules with a loving hand. It means you must be firm to uphold the boundary but compassionate enough to understand when empathy is required. For instance, if your child breaks a rule because they are upset, address the rule-breaking firmly but also show compassion by discussing what upset them. This approach teaches them that while their feelings are valid and cared for, the boundaries still need to be respected.

Respecting and Upholding Boundaries

As important as it is to set boundaries, it's equally crucial to respect them. This includes the boundaries set by others, including your children. Respecting their boundaries might look like knocking before entering their room or allowing them to have a say in their choices, such as clothes or extracurricular activities, within reasonable limits. By respecting their boundaries, you model how they should respect the boundaries of others.

Upholding your own boundaries is also crucial. Parents often put their needs and boundaries aside for the benefit of their children. However, showing that your boundaries are important teaches your children to respect not just your boundaries but the boundaries of others outside the family. For example, if you have set a boundary about not discussing work-related matters during family meals, stick to it and gently remind your family if they forget.

Setting boundaries with love is not about creating a regimented environment. Instead, it's about fostering a space where everyone feels safe, respected, and part of a loving family. By clearly communicating these boundaries, engaging your children in understanding them, and respecting each other's limits, you lay the foundation for a family dynamic that thrives on mutual respect and understanding. This approach does not merely solve immediate behavioral issues but deeply ingrains a sense of consideration and responsibility in your children, qualities they will carry into adulthood.

5.2 Establishing Family Values That Support Emotional Intelligence

Imagine your family as a garden, where values are the nutrients that enrich the soil, helping everything within it to thrive—these include the blossoming of emotional intelligence in your children, which encompasses empathy, respect, and resilience. Identifying and defining these core values is much like deciding what you want to grow in this garden. It requires thoughtful consideration and a clear vision of the kind of family dynamic you wish to cultivate. Begin by sitting down as a family and discussing what values are most important to each of you. Is it honesty? Kindness? Courage? Resilience? This discussion should be open and inclusive, allowing each family member, regardless of age, to voice what they feel is important. This helps identify values that truly reflect your family's beliefs and reinforces these values by giving everyone a sense of ownership and responsibility toward them.

Once these values are identified, the next step is integrating them into the fabric of your daily life, which can be both challenging and rewarding. It's about making these values visible and active rather than just a list on a piece of paper. For instance, if respect is a core value, demonstrate this through daily interactions. Use polite language, listen attentively when others speak, and show consideration for each other's feelings and opinions. Discuss these actions in family meetings, highlighting examples of how family members have shown respect in their actions. This not only serves as recognition but also reinforces the value through positive reinforcement.

Moreover, integrating these values into decision-making processes is crucial. This practice, known as value-based decision-making, involves using your family's values as a compass to guide your choices and actions. Let's say you're considering a job offer requiring you to work long hours and weekends. Suppose one of your family's core values is spending quality time with loved ones. In that case, you may decide that this job offer doesn't align with that value and decline it. On the other hand, if one of your family's values is financial stability, you may decide that the job offer is worth accepting despite the long hours. Using your family's values as a guidepost, you can make decisions consistent with what's truly important to you and your loved ones. This method not only helps in making decisions that feel right to everyone involved but also teaches children how to apply these values in their own decisions, seeing them as practical guides rather than abstract concepts.

Parents play a pivotal role in modeling these values. If you face challenges with resilience and a positive attitude, your children learn to do the same. Remember, teaching by example is one of the most potent education methods. It requires you to not only preach your family's values but to live them every day.

Establishing and nurturing these core values creates a strong foundation for your children's emotional intelligence. Through this ongoing process, your family becomes a strong, cohesive unit where each member feels valued and empowered to grow, supported by the shared values that you hold dear.

5.3 Co-Parenting and Blended Families: Navigating Emotional Landscapes

Navigating the dynamics of co-parenting and blending families introduces a complex palette of emotions and challenges that can test the fabric of any family structure. Whether negotiating weekend visits or integrating new step-siblings into the family, the key to harmonious relationships lies in the artful balance of open communication and consistent parenting approaches. In blended families, where children may be navigating loyalties to both biological and step-parents, the need for clarity and fairness in communication becomes even more pronounced. It's like being a conductor of a large orchestra where each player has a unique part to play; the goal is to create harmony, not uniformity.

For co-parents, establishing a rhythm of consistent communication can prevent a cacophony of mixed messages and emotional upheaval. This consistency isn't just about when and where children will spend holidays but also about maintaining a unified front on parenting decisions—from bedtime routines to screen time and behavioral consequences. It's crucial that you and your co-parent are on the same page, or at least reading from the same book, to provide a stable, predictable environment for your children. Regular check-ins, whether through face-to-face meetings or digital communication platforms, allow for sharing essential updates about your child's life and the opportunity to discuss any concerns or changes in family dynamics. These consistent updates help to preempt misunderstandings and conflicts that might arise from a lack of communication.

The emotional terrain of a blended family can sometimes feel like navigating a minefield, especially when managing loyalty conflicts that children might experience. These conflicts, often internal, can manifest as behavioral issues or emotional withdrawal and are rooted in a child's fear of betraying one parent by accepting another. To mitigate these conflicts, it's vital to create an environment where children feel free to love and respect all parental figures without feeling guilty or torn. This requires a delicate balance of encouraging relationships with all parents and step-parents while respecting the child's pace and feelings. Activities that foster family bonding can be beneficial, as can providing spaces where children can express their feelings openly, without fear of repercussion or disappointment.

Fostering a sense of unity and belonging within a blended family often involves consciously building a new family identity that celebrates individual members' uniqueness and the collective bond. This might include creating new family traditions or rituals everyone can partake in and enjoy, regardless of their role or biological ties. These shared experiences can be anchors of stability and joy amidst the changes and play a crucial role in building a cohesive family unit. It's also important to recognize and respect the existing bonds and traditions that children bring from their previous family setups. This acknowledgment helps children feel that their past and present are valued, not that one is being replaced by the other.

In every blended family's journey, the ultimate goal is to weave together the diverse threads of individual experiences, personalities, and histories into a tapestry that feels secure, loving, and inclusive. By prioritizing open communication, consistency in co-parenting approaches, sensitive handling of loyalty conflicts, and the deliberate creation of a unified family identity, you lay down the groundwork for a relationship dynamic that respects and celebrates each member's uniqueness while forging solid and enduring bonds. This approach not only smooths the emotional landscape of co-parenting and blended families but enriches it, turning challenges into opportunities for growth and deeper connection.

5.4 Family Rituals that Support Emotional Connection

Think of your family's daily interactions like the threads of a tapestry, each thread contributing to the overall strength and beauty of the family unit. Family rituals are these threads, vital in weaving a sense of belonging and emotional security. They are not just routines; they are meaningful practices that enhance emotional connection and provide comfort and stability amidst the chaos of everyday life. Whether it's a Friday night pizza party or a Sunday morning walk, these rituals create a predictable, joyous space that children—and adults—look forward to. They serve as emotional touchstones that can comfort and reassure, fostering a sense of continuity that is especially important in a world that often feels in flux.

Creating meaningful family rituals starts with understanding what makes an activity special. It's not about grand gestures; instead, it's the consistency and intention behind them that count. A ritual could be as simple as a bedtime story or a nightly gratitude discussion where each family member shares one thing they were thankful for that day. What's important is that these activities are consistent and inclusive, offering every family member a role and a voice. This regular engagement builds a foundation of shared experiences that strengthens family bonds and provides a comforting routine that all can rely on.

Let's explore some simple yet profound ritual ideas. Shared meals, for example, are a fantastic way to foster connection. Whether it's breakfasts before everyone heads out for the day or dinners where devices are turned off, these moments allow families to share food and conversations, ensuring everyone feels heard and connected. Bedtime stories, on the other hand, encourage literacy and provide a quiet moment for parents and children to cuddle and wind down from the day, making the transition to sleep calm and comforting. Weekend outings, be it to a park, a museum, or a local market, offer refreshing breaks from routine, creating memories and experiences that become cherished over time.

Customizing these rituals to fit your family's unique interests and schedules makes them more engaging and sustainable. If your family loves the outdoors, perhaps a weekly hike or bike ride could become a cherished ritual. If creativity is a shared passion, a weekend craft hour where everyone makes something could be your go-to ritual. The key is to choose activities that resonate with the interests of your family members, ensuring everyone looks forward to these times together. Also, consider your family's schedule. It's essential to choose rituals that fit naturally into your lives without feeling like a burden; otherwise, they're likely to fall by the wayside.

As your children grow and family dynamics evolve, so should your rituals. This flexibility helps maintain their relevance and enjoyment. For instance, the bedtime stories that delight your toddler might transition into a family book club as your children grow into avid readers. Similarly, a weekly game night might evolve from simple board games to more complex games or outdoor sports as the kids grow older and seek more challenges. Recognizing and adapting to these changes keeps family rituals fresh and engaging, ensuring they continue to serve their purpose of bonding and emotional comfort.

Another powerful aspect of family rituals is their use in celebrating big and small successes. Holding regular family meetings where achievements like a good grade, a new skill learned, or progress in self-regulation are acknowledged and celebrated reinforces positive behaviors and boosts morale. These celebrations can be simple, like a special dessert for the achiever or ten minutes of extra bedtime stories. What matters is the act of recognition and the message it sends—that each family member's efforts and successes are valued and celebrated.

Incorporating these rituals into the fabric of your family life creates a rhythm of connection and joy, enhancing emotional bonds and providing stable, comforting routines amidst life's unpredictabilities. By choosing, adapting, and evolving these rituals to suit your family's changing needs and interests, you ensure they remain a cherished part of your family's life, weaving a strong, supportive family dynamic that nurtures everyone involved.

5.5 Creating a Safe Space for Feelings

Imagine your home as a sanctuary where every family member feels secure enough to express their deepest feelings without fear of judgment or dismissal. This environment, vital for emotional well-being, requires cultivating open communication and validating each person's feelings. Think of it as building a garden where emotions, like plants, can bloom safely and beautifully, nurtured by understanding and empathy.

Fostering Open Communication

Creating an environment that encourages open communication starts with you as a parent. It's about being approachable and available. When your child comes to you with a concern, no matter how small it may seem, it's important to stop what you're doing and listen actively. This shows that you value their feelings and thoughts. You can enhance this open atmosphere by establishing regular family meetings where everyone is invited to share their feelings and thoughts about various family issues or their personal experiences. These meetings should be a safe space where emotions are not only expressed but also respected. Make it clear that these gatherings are not about problem-solving or judgment but about understanding and supporting each other. This practice not only helps in clearing up misunderstandings but also strengthens the bonds of trust and intimacy within the family.

Validating Feelings

Validation is the cornerstone of building emotional safety. It involves acknowledging and accepting your family members' feelings as real and significant, regardless of whether or not you understand or agree with them. Validation can be as simple as saying, "I see that you're really upset about this," or "It sounds like you had a tough day." Avoid minimizing their feelings with phrases like "It's not a big deal" or "You're just being sensitive." Instead, show empathy and try to understand the situation from their perspective. This approach does not mean you are agreeing with their perspectives or behaviors, but you are acknowledging their feelings as valid. This validation helps soothe distress and make your child feel heard and understood, which is crucial for their emotional development.

Understanding Triggers

Helping children understand what triggers their emotions involves exploring the feelings, thoughts, and situations that precede an emotional reaction. For instance, if a child throws a tantrum every time they need to do homework, delve deeper to discover what about the situation is upsetting them. Is the work too challenging, or are they afraid of making mistakes? Understanding these triggers can help them manage their reactions better. Teach them to recognize these triggers and articulate what they are feeling. Phrases like, "When I have to do math homework, I feel stupid," can be starting points for addressing more profound self-esteem issues and academic pressure.

Teaching Healthy Expression

Expressing emotions healthily is a skill that children need to learn early. Encourage verbal expression by teaching them words for different emotions and how to express their feelings appropriately. For instance, instead of hitting when angry, they can say, "I am really mad right now!" Additionally, creative outlets such as drawing, journaling, or playing music can be therapeutic ways for children to deal with complex emotions. Physical activity, like running or dancing, can also be a healthy way for children to manage feelings like anger or frustration. These activities not only help in expressing emotions in the moment but also build resilience and emotional regulation skills over time.

Coping Mechanisms

Introduce age-appropriate coping mechanisms that children can turn to when they feel overwhelmed. Techniques like deep breathing, counting to ten, or visualizing a calm place can be effective for younger children. Older children might benefit from more structured approaches like mindfulness meditation or writing in a journal. Teach these techniques during calm moments, and encourage your children to use them when they start feeling overwhelmed. Over time, these coping mechanisms can become second nature, helping them manage their emotions more effectively.

Creating this safe space for feelings in your family involves continuous effort and patience. It requires you to be both a teacher and a student—teaching your children about emotional intelligence while also learning from their unique perspectives and experiences. By fostering the elements in this sub-chapter, you equip your family with the tools to navigate the complexities of their emotions and support each other through them. This foundation of emotional safety and literacy is a gift that will serve your children well throughout their lives, enriching their relationships and enhancing their overall well-being.

5.6 The Role of Play in Emotional Regulation and Bonding

Play isn't just a fundamental way for children to pass the time; it's a vital tool for emotional regulation and a bonding agent for families. Think of play as a language through which children communicate their feelings and learn to navigate their emotions. It provides a safe outlet for expressing themselves—whether through the roles they choose in pretend play or the strategies they devise in a board game. This natural form of expression helps children process complex feelings and situations, making play an essential element in their emotional development.

When selecting play activities that enhance emotional regulation, consider games that require a mix of strategy and patience. Board games like chess or cooperative games where players work towards a common goal can teach children how to plan, anticipate consequences, and react to the game's ups and downs. These games mimic real-life situations where emotions might run high—like dealing with an unexpected setback or enjoying the thrill of a hard-earned success. By navigating these in the safe context of play, children learn to regulate their emotions, enhancing their ability to handle similar situations in real life.

Incorporating play into family life doesn't have to be a structured affair. It can be as simple as impromptu tickle fights on a lazy Sunday morning or building a family fort on a rainy afternoon. These playful moments are not only fun but are crucial for strengthening family bonds and improving communication. They create memories and traditions that children cherish well into adulthood. Moreover, when parents actively participate in play, not just as supervisors but as co-players, they send a powerful message. It shows kids that their world is important and worthy of adult attention, which can significantly boost their self-esteem and sense of security.

Outdoor play is another fantastic way to incorporate physical activity with emotional regulation. Activities like hiking, cycling, or even a simple game of tag can help burn off the pent-up energy that might otherwise manifest as anxiety or aggression. Physical activities also stimulate the production of endorphins, the body's natural mood enhancers, improving the family's overall mood and emotional climate. For a creative twist, engaging in arts and crafts projects as a family can offer a calm and focused outlet for emotions, allowing for gentle discussions about feelings and experiences as you paint, draw, or build together.

Reflecting on play experiences provides a golden opportunity for emotional growth and learning. After a game night or a family outing, take a few moments to discuss what happened during the play, what everyone felt at different points, and what can be learned from those experiences. Did someone get frustrated when they lost? How did they handle that frustration? Was it challenging to work together during a cooperative game? What strategies worked well, and what could be improved? These discussions can help children connect their play experiences with real-life skills, such as coping with disappointment, working collaboratively, or standing up for themselves in respectful ways.

Through play, families can create a dynamic environment where children feel loved and supported in exploring their emotions and developing essential life skills. By actively participating in play, choosing activities that foster emotional growth, and reflecting on these experiences together, you enrich your family's emotional landscape. This helps children learn to regulate their emotions through enjoyable activities and deepens the family's emotional connection.

We have explored various aspects of building strong family bonds, from setting boundaries with love to practicing family rituals. Each subchapter has provided valuable insights and practical strategies. We have learned how to establish family values, navigate the emotional complexities of blended families, and create safe spaces where feelings are respected and embraced. At the core of our discussion lies the transformative power of play, which is a universal language that helps bridge the gap between generations and fosters emotional regulation. As we move on to the next chapter, we will continue to build on these foundations and delve deeper into everyday actions that can help with self-regulation and mindfulness.

Make a Difference with Your Review

Unlock the Power of Generosity

"The greatest good you can do for another is not just to share your riches, but to reveal to him his own."

-Benjamin Disraeli

People who give without expectation live longer, happier lives and make more money. So if we've got a shot at that during our time together, I'm gonna try.

To make that happen, I have a question for you... Would you help someone you've never met, even if you never got credit for it?

Who is this person you ask? They are like you. Or, at least, like you used to be. Less experienced, wanting to make a difference, and needing help, but unsure where to look.

My mission is to make self-regulation accessible to everyone. Everything I do stems from that mission. And, the only way for me to accomplish that mission is by reaching...well...everyone.

This is where you come in. Most people do, in fact, judge a book by its cover (and its reviews). So here's my ask on behalf of a struggling parent you've never met:

Please help that parent by leaving this book a review.

Your gift costs no money and takes less than 60 seconds to make real but it can change a fellow parent's life forever. Your review could help...

...one more parent find calm in the chaos.

...one more family start their day with smiles.

...one more child learn to handle emotions.

...one more household feel more connected.

To get that 'feel good' feeling and help this person for real, all you have to do is...and it takes less than 60 seconds... Leave a review.

Simply scan the QR code below to leave your review:

[https://www.amazon.com/review/review-your-purchases/?asin=BOOKASIN]

If you feel good about helping a faceless parent, you are my kind of person. Welcome to the club. You're one of us.

I'm that much more excited to help you achieve a calmer, more connected family life faster and easier than you can possibly imagine. You'll love the strategies I'm about to share in the coming chapters.

Thank you from the bottom of my heart. Now, back to our regularly scheduled program-ming.

PS - Fun fact: If you provide something of value to another person, it makes you more valuable to them. If you'd like goodwill straight from another parent - and you believe this book will help them - send this book their way.

Chapter Six

Daily Practices for Self-Regulation

I magine it's early morning, and instead of the usual rush and hustle, your home is filled with a sense of calm and readiness. The kids are getting ready without being told twice, breakfast is a time of togetherness rather than a battleground, and you all leave the house with smiles instead of stress lines. This isn't a scene from an idealized movie; it's entirely achievable with the proper morning routines. This section of our journey through mindful parenting zeroes in on transforming your mornings from chaotic to harmonious, setting a positive tone for the day.

6.1 Morning Routines that Reduce Stress and Increase harmony

Structured Start

The magic of a structured morning routine lies in its ability to significantly reduce stress for both you and your children. By establishing a predictable series of events each morning, you eliminate a lot of the chaos and uncertainty that can fuel tension and anxiety. Start by defining what needs to be done and who is responsible for each task. One child may be in charge of feeding the pet while another packs the snacks. Maybe your role is to oversee the brushing of teeth and hair. Whatever the tasks, make sure everyone knows their responsibilities. This clarity not only makes the morning flow more smoothly but also helps children feel competent and capable, boosting their confidence and easing stress.

Mindful Mornings

Introducing mindfulness practices into your morning routine can dramatically alter the day's tone. Even something as simple as starting the day with a few deep breaths together can center and calm the entire family. Consider integrating a short meditation or a gentle yoga session into your morning schedule. These practices don't have to be lengthy; even a few minutes can make a significant difference. Apps and online videos geared toward families can guide you if you're new to these practices. The key is consistency and making it a non-negotiable part of your morning, much like brushing your teeth. Over time, these moments of calm can become a cherished part of your family's routine, cherished islands of peace in the daily rush.

Morning routine idea: RISE

Revitalize your energy with a quick morning stretch.

Inspire yourself (by listening to an uplifting song, podcast, or video, reading a passage from a favorite book, thinking of three things you're grateful for, etc.)

Set your top priorities for the day.

Exhale deeply a few times to start your day with calm and focus.

Preparation Tips

One of the best strategies to reduce morning stress is preparation the night before. Encourage your children to pick out their clothes, pack their school bags, and even help prepare lunchboxes before bedtime. Discuss the next day's schedule to ensure everyone knows what to expect and any special items they need to remember. You can also prepare breakfast settings or ingredients to save time in the morning. These simple acts of preparation can prevent many morning mishaps and misunderstandings, smoothing the path for everyone.

Family Meetings

While it might seem unusual to think of having family meetings in the morning, a brief gathering to set daily intentions can be incredibly powerful. This doesn't have to be formal or lengthy; just a few minutes during breakfast or right before everyone heads out the door can suffice. Use this time to sync up on everyone's schedules, any concerns or special events for the day, and perhaps share a positive affirmation or goal. This practice not only keeps everyone informed but also fosters a sense of teamwork and support. It's a way to remind each family member that they're part of a caring and connected unit, which can be incredibly reassuring, especially on more challenging days.

Incorporating these strategies into your morning routine can transform how your family starts the day. By reducing stress and increasing harmony, you set everyone up for success, both emotionally and practically. These morning practices are not just about getting out the door on time; they're about nurturing a family dynamic that values mindfulness, preparedness, and cooperation. As you weave these practices into the fabric of your daily life, you'll likely find that their benefits extend far beyond the morning hours, influencing your family's overall tone and emotional health.

6.2 Incorporating Mindfulness into Your Daily Parenting Tasks

Mindfulness, a term often associated with meditation and wellness, is a powerful tool for parents. It's not just about personal tranquility but about transforming your interactions with your children, especially in challenging situations. By observing your current experiences (emotions, sensations, and thoughts) without judgment, you can maintain emotional balance and avoid being overwhelmed. This is particularly beneficial in the demanding parenting role, helping you stay present and connected with your children.

Embracing mindfulness doesn't require hours of silent meditation. It can be seamlessly integrated into your daily activities, making it a practical and effective strategy for even the busiest parents. Here are four simple ideas that can be practiced almost anywhere in your day.

1. Mindful listening

Start with something as simple as mindful listening (which is pretty much a synonym for active listening, which we discussed in Chapter 4). This practice involves entirely focusing on your child as they speak without planning your following response or allowing your mind to wander to the myriad of tasks awaiting you. This undivided attention helps you better understand your child's thoughts and feelings. It strengthens your connection, showing them that they are valued and heard.

Here is a concrete example. Imagine you're sitting down for dinner, and your child starts talking about their day. Instead of nodding absentmindedly while you think about what chores you must finish, you focus entirely on their words, facial expressions, and tone. You might notice a slight hesitation when they mention a friend or a sparkle in their eyes when they talk about a new book they read. This level of attentiveness allows you to grasp not just the surface details but the more profound revelations of your child's experiences and feelings.

2. Mindful observation

Another practical mindfulness technique is mindful observation, which you can practice during routine activities like walking to the park or driving your kids to school. It involves consciously noting the details of your environment—the color of the sky, the shape of clouds, the feel of the steering wheel under your hands. This practice pulls your mind away from worries and plans, anchoring you in the present moment. It's an excellent way to model calmness and presence to your children, showing them how to appreciate the simple joys of everyday life.

Here is an example from another line of thought. If you observe your child struggling to build a block tower, resist the immediate impulse to fix the problem. Instead, watch how they handle the frustration or challenge. Do they try a different strategy? Do they ask for help? This observation allows you to appreciate their growing abilities to solve problems and manage emotions. It gives your child the space to learn from their own experiences.

3. Mindful walking

It can be a game changer. It involves fully concentrating on the experience of walking, noticing the sensation of your feet touching the ground, the rhythm of your breath, and the sounds around you. This can be done during a walk to the park with your kids or even walking to your car after a grocery run.

4. Mindful eating

It's another practice that can transform a daily activity into a mindful ritual. It involves paying full attention to the eating experience, noticing the textures, flavors, and smells of your food, and appreciating the nourishment it provides.

Lastly, integrating mindfulness into everyday activities like cooking, cleaning, and driving can turn these routine tasks into opportunities for calm and connection. For example, you might invite your child to help you cook dinner. As you both engage in the task, describe what you're doing and why, from the spices you choose to how you chop vegetables. Encourage them to be present, perhaps by focusing on the ingredients' textures or the cooking sounds. Not only does this make the task more enjoyable, but it also teaches your child how to apply mindfulness in everyday situations. Similarly, when cleaning, you could focus on the satisfaction of seeing a tidy space emerge, or when driving, you could discuss the changing scenery or play a game of spotting different types of vehicles. Bringing mindfulness to these everyday actions transforms them from mundane tasks into moments of discovery and togetherness.

The impact of these mindfulness practices on your relationship with your children can be profound. Being fully present makes you more likely to respond effectively to your children's needs and emotions. This presence builds a foundation of trust and understanding, crucial components of a solid parent-child relationship. Children feel more secure and valued when they see their parents genuinely engaged in their worlds, whether sharing a story about their day or seeking comfort after a setback. This secure attachment fosters greater openness, reduces behavioral problems, and enhances mutual empathy, setting the stage for a lifetime of healthy emotional interactions.

Incorporating mindfulness into your parenting approach doesn't just help during smooth, everyday interactions; it becomes invaluable during times of stress and conflict. When tensions rise—say, during a disagreement over homework or bedtime routines—mindful presence allows you to approach the situation with a clear, calm mind. Instead of reacting hastily or letting emotions get the best of you, mindfulness will enable you to breathe, assess, and address the issue thoughtfully.

By integrating mindfulness into your daily life and embracing it as a key element of your parenting toolkit, you create an environment of calm, presence, and connectedness. This not only enhances your own well-being but also deeply enriches your family life, making each interaction more meaningful and each day a little smoother. As you continue to practice and model mindfulness, you instill these values in your children, equipping them with the tools to navigate their emotions and relationships effectively now and in the future. However, it's important to remember that mindfulness is not a magic solution to all parenting challenges. It's a practice that requires some time and effort, and it's just one tool among many that can help you become a more effective and connected parent.

6.3 Evening Wind-Down Rituals for You and Your Child

As the day draws to a close, creating a tranquil environment for you and your children can substantially enhance the quality of your family's rest and overall well-being. Integrating evening wind-down rituals not only helps in transitioning from the day's hustle to peaceful night-time but also in strengthening bonds and nurturing emotional health. Among these rituals, relaxation techniques play a pivotal role. One effective method for parents and children is guided imagery, where you and your child visualize a calming scene or story. This could involve imagining a gentle stream in a beautiful forest or picturing yourself floating on clouds. You can find guided imagery scripts online or even create your own. This practice not only soothes the mind but also provides a fantastic opportunity for bonding as you embark on these tranquil journeys together.

Another excellent relaxation technique is progressive muscle relaxation. This involves tensing and then relaxing different muscle groups in the body. You can guide your child through this process by starting at the toes and slowly working up to the forehead. For each part of the body, hold the tension for about five seconds and then release. This not only helps release physical tension but also teaches children to recognize when they are feeling physically tense and how to manage it. Making this a bedtime ritual can not only improve sleep quality but also equip your child with a valuable tool to manage stress.

In today's digital age, where screens are an integral part of our lives, instituting a digital detox during evening hours can significantly benefit your family's night-time routine. The blue light emitted by screens can interfere with the natural production of melatonin, the hormone responsible for regulating sleep, making it harder to fall asleep. By setting a specific time each evening after which no screens are allowed, you help everyone in the family unwind naturally. During this screen-free time, you can engage in other relaxing activities like reading books, doing puzzles, or simply chatting about the day. This helps wind down effectively and ensures your time together is meaningful and connecting.

Reflective journaling is another enriching evening ritual that can benefit both you and your children. It involves writing down thoughts, feelings, and events of the day, providing a therapeutic way to process daily experiences and emotions. Younger children who may not yet be able to write extensively can draw or use stickers to express their day's experiences and emotions. This not only helps in developing their emotional expression but also enhances their creative skills. For parents, reflective journaling offers a quiet moment to introspect and unwind, potentially revealing insights into your parenting and personal growth. Encouraging this practice can foster a habit of self-reflection and mindfulness among your children, equipping them with skills to introspectively navigate their emotions and experiences throughout life.

These evening rituals not only aid in better sleep and reduced stress but also strengthen the emotional bonds within your family by providing structured, calming activities that promote closeness and communication.

6.4 Creating a Self-Regulation Plan for High-Stress Times

In the ebb and flow of family life, certain periods stand out as particularly challenging. Think of times like the holidays, with their whirlwind of activities and expectations, or transitions like moving to a new home or welcoming a new family member. During such high-stress times, having a robust self-regulation plan can be your anchor, helping you navigate these waters with more grace and less stress.

Developing a personalized self-regulation plan begins with understanding what these high-stress times look like for you and your family. Each family's experience is unique, so tailor your approach to your specific circumstances and needs. Start by mapping out periods you anticipate will be stressful. For instance, if you know that the start of the school year is a hectic time, you can begin preparations earlier in the summer. As part of this plan, set clear, manageable goals for each period. These might include maintaining a regular sleep schedule for everyone in the family, ensuring healthy meals are planned and prepped in advance, or setting aside quiet time each evening to wind down.

Next, consider the coping mechanisms that work best for you and your children. It's helpful to have a toolbox of strategies that you can adapt to different situations. This might include breathing exercises for immediate stress relief, a set of affirmations for boosting morale, or physical activities like a family walk after dinner to dissipate tension. It's also wise to have some quick relaxation techniques up your sleeve, like listening to calming music or doing a few stretches, which can be especially useful when time is limited. Encourage each family member to identify personal coping strategies that they feel will help them during these times, and discuss as a family how you can support each other in using these techniques.

Identifying and utilizing support systems is an often overlooked but crucial aspect of your plan. This might involve delegating tasks to other family members, arranging playdates or childcare swaps with friends to give you a breather, or even seeking professional help like counseling or therapy if the stress feels unmanageable. Remember, asking for help is a sign of strength, not weakness. It shows a commitment to maintaining your family's well-being. Make a list of people—family, friends, neighbors, professionals—whom you can contact during these times, and keep their contact information handy.

Finally, the importance of regularly reviewing and revising your plan cannot be overstated. What works in one season of life may not be as effective in another. Make it a point to reflect on the effectiveness of your plan after each stressful period. Discuss as a family what helped and what didn't, and adjust accordingly. This not only improves the plan but also reinforces to your children the importance of flexibility and continuous learning in managing stress.

Creating and maintaining a self-regulation plan for high-stress times isn't just about reducing stress; it's about empowering your family to handle life's challenges with resilience and togetherness. By planning ahead, choosing effective coping mechanisms, leveraging your support network, and staying flexible, you equip yourself and your children with the tools to manage stress more effectively, making room for more joy and less anxiety in your family life.

As we wrap up this chapter, remember the strategies we explored. They are relevant not just in times of stress but also in our everyday lives, enhancing our ability to navigate the ordinary and extraordinary challenges of parenting. Moving forward, the next chapter will guide you in further strengthening your family's resilience and emotional intelligence.

Chapter Seven

Addressing Specific Challenges with Self-Regulation

Imagine you're in the middle of a busy grocery store, your shopping list in one hand and your toddler's hand in the other. Suddenly, out of nowhere, your little one's mood flips. The once cheerful chatter turns into loud sobs and stomping feet over a candy bar you said no to. Everyone's eyes seem to turn on you, watching how you'll navigate this public spectacle. Moments like these test the very fibers of your patience and self-regulation. This chapter is about turning such challenging situations into opportunities for teaching, learning, and growing—both for you and your child.

7.1 Dealing with Public Tantrums Mindfully

Staying Calm

The first step in dealing with a public tantrum is managing your own emotional response. It's natural to feel embarrassed, frustrated, or even angry when your child starts screaming in a public place. However, maintaining your calm is crucial, not only for dealing with the situation effectively but also for modeling composed behavior for your child. Deep breathing, previously explained, can be a lifesaver here. You can also try the "4-7-8" technique: breathe in quietly through your nose for 4 seconds, hold the breath for 7 seconds, and exhale completely through your mouth for 8 seconds. This technique (invented by Dr. Andrew Weil) helps reduce anxiety. It brings your focus back to managing the situation at hand.

Visualizing a calm place can also help maintain your composure. Picture yourself in a peaceful setting—perhaps a quiet beach at sunset or a cozy corner of your home. This mental shift can provide a brief respite from the stress of the moment, allowing you to approach the situation with a cooler head.

Distraction and Diversion

Once you've managed to steady your nerves, the next step is to address your child. Often, young children use tantrums to express themselves when they can't articulate their feelings in words. Offering a distraction can help shift their focus from the trigger. Point out something interesting in the surroundings, or propose a fun activity like playing a game of "I spy." Sometimes, all it takes is a new focus to break the tantrum cycle.

If distraction doesn't work, consider diversion. This involves offering alternatives that are acceptable to you. For instance, if the tantrum is about not buying a toy, divert your child's attention to choosing a fruit for dessert instead. It's about finding a compromise that shifts their focus and satisfies their need for agency.

Post-Tantrum Discussion

Once the storm has passed, discussing the event with your child is essential. Find a quiet moment when you're both calm and explain why public outbursts aren't acceptable. Use simple language that your child can understand, and encourage them to express what triggered their behavior. Discuss emotions and alternative ways to handle them. For example, if they were upset about not getting the toy, you could teach them to say "I'm sad" instead of crying. These discussions are crucial for emotional development, helping your child learn appropriate ways of expressing their feelings.

Managing Judgment

Dealing with the judgment of bystanders can be one of the most challenging parts of handling a public tantrum. Remember, most parents have been in similar situations, and their judgments are often not as harsh as you might fear. If someone offers advice or comments, respond politely, "Thank you" or "We're handling it." Sometimes, acknowledging the situation can alleviate the perceived pressure from onlookers. Focus on your child and what they need in that moment rather than the opinions of those around you. Your priority is your child's well-being and learning, not the judgments of strangers.

Handling public tantrums is as much about teaching your child as it is about maintaining your own emotional regulation. By staying calm, using distraction and diversion effectively, discussing the tantrum afterward, and managing external judgments, you turn these challenging moments into opportunities for growth and learning.

7.2 Technology and Screen Time: Setting Boundaries with Emotional Wisdom

In today's digital age, screens are ubiquitous in family life, offering both incredible resources and significant challenges. The key to harnessing the benefits of technology while minimizing its downsides lies in setting thoughtful, age-appropriate boundaries. For children whose brains and social skills are still developing, understanding how to interact with technology in a healthy way is crucial. As a parent, you can guide them by establishing clear and consistent rules about screen time.

Setting Healthy Boundaries

The first step in establishing healthy screen time habits is to create clear guidelines appropriate for your child's age and maturity level. For younger children, this might mean limiting screen time to educational content or short, supervised sessions with apps that encourage learning and creativity. As children grow, introduce them to more interactive tools like educational games to enhance their problem-solving and critical-thinking skills. However, limiting entertainment screen time is crucial, ensuring it doesn't replace vital activities like physical play, reading, and face-to-face social interaction.

For older children and teenagers, who may need to use screens for schoolwork, set boundaries that help them differentiate between work and leisure. Encourage them to take regular breaks to prevent digital eye strain and ensure they balance screen time with other activities. One effective strategy is using tech-free zones in the home, such as bedrooms and dining areas, which can help children (and adults) disconnect and engage more fully in family time and restful sleep.

Negotiating Screen Time

Involving your children in discussions and decisions about screen time can empower them and make the boundaries more effective. Sit down with your children and talk about why limits are necessary, discussing the impact of too much screen time on health and well-being. Let them share their thoughts and feelings about these rules, and consider their input when setting limits. This could mean negotiating specific times when they can watch TV or play video games, which can be adjusted based on their daily schedule and responsibilities. By involving them in decision-making, you help them understand and accept the rules and teach them essential self-regulation and negotiation skills.

The Impact of Screen Time on Emotional Well-being

Excessive screen time can significantly affect children's emotional and physical health. It's been linked to increased risks of obesity, sleep problems, and decreased performance in school. On the emotional front, too much screen time can lead to feelings of anxiety and depression, especially if it replaces real-life interactions with friends and family. To mitigate these effects, encourage regular breaks during long periods of screen use and ensure screens are turned off at least an hour before bedtime to help them wind down effectively.

It's also essential to monitor the content your children are exposed to during their screen time. Violent or otherwise inappropriate content can have adverse effects on young minds. Use parental controls to ensure they're accessing age-appropriate content and discuss the content they're consuming. This not only helps protect them from harmful material but also gives you insight into their interests and concerns, which can be great starting points for meaningful conversations.

Modeling Technology Use

Children learn a lot by watching their parents, so you must model healthy screen habits yourself. Show your children how you balance technology in your own life and discuss the choices you make, such as not checking emails during family meals or prioritizing offline hobbies and activities. Your behavior sets a benchmark for their actions, and by practicing what you preach, you reinforce the family's screen time rules as mandates and shared values.

Encouraging Alternative Activities

To balance screen time, actively encourage activities that don't involve screens. Depending on your child's interests, these could include sports, reading, arts and crafts, or playing musical instruments. Not only do these activities provide necessary breaks from screens, but they also support healthy development in areas such as physical fitness, creativity, and social skills. Plan regular family activities that are engaging and fun, such as hiking, board games, or cooking together, which can help strengthen family bonds and show that fun and relaxation don't always require a digital component.

By setting thoughtful boundaries, involving your children in the process, understanding the impacts of screen time, modeling healthy habits, and encouraging a wide variety of activities, you can ensure that technology serves as a positive force in your family's life. These strategies help foster an environment where children can enjoy the benefits of digital tools while developing a healthy, balanced approach to their use.

7.3 Homework Battles: Applying Emotional Intelligence for Peaceful Solutions

When the word "homework" becomes a source of tension and dread in your household, it's time to rethink your approach. Understanding the root of homework frustrations is crucial for both you and your children. Often, these feelings stem from a mismatch between your child's expectations and abilities and the demands of the tasks at hand. For children, feelings of inadequacy or fear of failure can quickly turn a simple assignment into a battleground. From your perspective, frustration might arise from seeing your child struggle or feeling pressure for them to succeed academically. Recognizing these emotional undercurrents is the first step in transforming homework from a conflict zone into a constructive part of the day.

Creating a conducive environment for homework is about more than just a quiet space. It involves crafting an atmosphere that supports concentration and learning. Start by designating a specific area for homework free from distractions like television and household noise. This space should be well-lit and stocked with all the necessary supplies like pencils, paper, and calculators, so no last-minute scramble can cause stress. Consider the ergonomics of the workspace, too; a comfortable chair and a desk at the right height can make a big difference in how long your child can focus. Most importantly, make this area a phone-free zone for your child and yourself to set a tone of focused attention.

Establishing a consistent homework routine can also significantly reduce stress. Decide on a set time each day for homework, allowing some wiggle room depending on the day's activities. This predictability helps children mentally prepare for the task and transitions them more smoothly from playtime or relaxation into work mode. Incorporate breaks into this routine, especially for longer assignments. Just like adults, children need downtime to prevent burnout and maintain productivity. Try the Pomodoro Technique: 25 minutes of focused work followed by a 5-minute break. During breaks, encourage activities that truly feel like a rest from work, like stretching, grabbing a snack, or stepping outside for a few minutes of fresh air.

Rewards can be a part of your homework routine, but it's important to use them wisely. Instead of bribing your child to complete assignments with promises of screen time or treats, use rewards to celebrate the completion of homework milestones. For instance, finishing a week's worth of homework on time could be marked with a special family game night or a choice of what's for dinner. This approach reinforces positive behavior without making the reward the sole focus of doing homework.

Providing empathetic support during homework time means being available to help without taking over. It's about guiding your child to find answers rather than giving them outright. If they're stuck, resist the urge to solve the problem for them. Instead, ask guiding questions that lead them to figure it out on their own. For example, if they're perplexed by a math problem, ask, "What's the first step in solving this kind of equation?" If they're writing an essay, encourage them to outline their thoughts before they begin. This supportive approach helps build their confidence and skills, showing them they can tackle challenges independently.

Additionally, acknowledge the effort they put into their work, not just the outcomes. Praise their dedication and resilience, especially when struggling with complex material. This validation can be incredibly motivating for children, reinforcing the value of hard work and perseverance over simply getting the correct answers.

By understanding the emotional aspects of homework, creating a supportive environment, establishing a consistent routine, and offering empathetic support, you can help your child navigate homework challenges with greater ease and effectiveness. This approach not only eases homework battles but also fosters skills and attitudes that will benefit your child far beyond their school years.

7.4 Navigating Sibling Rivalry with Calm and Fairness

Sibling rivalry is as old as the stories of Cain and Abel. While most sibling disputes don't reach biblical proportions, they can still disrupt the harmony of your household. Whether it's a fight over a toy or arguments about privacy, navigating these conflicts with fairness and calm can turn these challenging moments into opportunities for teaching essential life skills such as empathy, sharing, and communication.

Acknowledging Feelings

When tensions arise between siblings, it's crucial to acknowledge each child's feelings first. This validation is critical to helping them feel heard and understood, which can diffuse intense emotions and prevent the situation from escalating. For example, when one child is upset because another won't share a game, it's important to express understanding to both children. You might tell the upset child, "I see you're really disappointed because you wanted a turn with the game." To the other child, you could express, "I understand that it's hard to stop playing when you're having fun." This kind of acknowledgment doesn't mean you agree with their behavior, but it does show that you recognize and care about their feelings. It's about striking a balance where neither child feels sidelined, but both feel supported, laying a groundwork where emotions are respected and discussed openly.

Fair Conflict Resolution

Once emotions are acknowledged, guiding children through a process of fair conflict resolution can teach them how to negotiate and compromise, skills that are valuable both in and outside the family. Begin by helping them define the problem in their own words. Ask each child to express their perspective and listen to the other without interrupting. This practice fosters mutual understanding and respect. Next, encourage them to brainstorm solutions together. This could involve taking turns, playing together, or finding another game. It's important to steer them towards solutions that involve compromise; for instance, setting a timer for turns can be an excellent way for both to feel they are getting a fair share of playtime. Your role here is to facilitate the discussion, help clarify misunderstandings, and ensure the proposed solutions are fair to everyone involved. By involving children in resolving their disputes, you empower them to handle conflicts independently in the future, fostering a sense of accomplishment and self-efficacy.

Individual Attention

In families with multiple children, rivalry often stems from competition for parental attention. Each child is unique and may require different types of attention and support. Make it a priority to spend one-on-one time with each child, engaging in activities catering to their interests and needs. This could be as simple as reading a book to one child based on their interests while taking another out for a walk to discuss what's on their mind. These moments are crucial for bonding and making each child feel valued and loved as an individual. They provide a safe space for children to express concerns or issues they might not feel comfortable sharing in front of siblings. During these times, focus fully on the child you are with, making them feel that they have your undivided attention. This practice can significantly reduce feelings of jealousy and competition, as each child sees that they have their special time with you.

Navigating sibling rivalry with calmness and fairness involves acknowledging each child's feelings, guiding them through resolving conflicts together, and ensuring each child receives individual attention. These actions don't just resolve conflicts; they teach your children valuable interpersonal skills and strengthen their bonds with each other and with you. By handling sibling rivalry in this way, you help cultivate a family environment where children feel safe, heard, and equally loved, laying a solid foundation for them to grow into well-rounded individuals who value and respect one another's differences and abilities.

7.5 Maintaining Patience During Bedtime Routines

Bedtime should not feel like a battleground but rather a peaceful close to the day, a quiet time that helps your child transition from the day's excitement to the calm of the night. Establishing a consistent, calming bedtime routine is key. This means having a set series of steps that signal your child that the day is winding down, preparing their mind and body for sleep. Whether it's brushing teeth, changing into pajamas, or reading a bedtime story, these activities should be predictable and comforting. Consistency helps your child know what to expect each evening. It aids in setting their internal clock, making it easier for them to fall asleep and wake up naturally at the same time each day.

Incorporating mindfulness or relaxation techniques can significantly enhance this bedtime routine. Techniques such as guided relaxation or gentle yoga poses designed for children can be an excellent way to help your little one release the physical and mental tensions of the day. You might guide them through imagining their favorite place, encouraging them to visualize the sights, sounds, and smells, or lead them through gentle stretches and poses that mimic animals or nature. These activities not only promote relaxation but also provide a perfect opportunity for bonding, giving you a few moments of quiet connection with your child. You can refer to Chapter 6.3 for more bedtime rituals.

Addressing bedtime procrastination is another crucial aspect of creating a smooth bedtime routine. It's common for children to want to delay going to bed by asking for just one more story, another glass of water, or one last trip to the bathroom. While meeting your child's needs is important, it's also necessary to set clear boundaries and consequences around bedtime. Start by understanding why your child is procrastinating—is it because they aren't tired, they're afraid of missing out, or perhaps they're actually scared of the dark? Once you understand the root cause, you can address it directly, perhaps by adjusting nap times, adding a nightlight to their room, or establishing a "winding down" period before bed that helps them transition more gradually into sleep time.

Quality time during the bedtime routine can make this part of the day something your child looks forward to rather than resists. Spend these moments fully engaged with your child, without distractions from phones or other devices. This might involve reading together, talking about the day, singing a quiet song, or simply cuddling. This helps your child feel loved and secure and fills their need for your attention in a positive, calm way, making them less likely to seek it through negative behaviors like procrastination.

By establishing a consistent routine, using relaxation techniques, addressing procrastination wisely, and spending quality time, bedtime can become a cherished part of the day for you and your child. It's about ending the day with peace and love, ensuring your child drifts off to sleep feeling safe, relaxed, and connected.

7.6 Responding to Back Talk without Escalation

When your child responds with a sharp "Whatever!" or a defiant "You can't make me!" it's not just challenging—it's an invitation to peer into a deeper level of communication that goes beyond mere words. Backtalk, often seen as a hallmark of the teenage years but also prevalent among younger children, is typically a manifestation of a child's growing desire for independence and control over their own decisions. It can also be a sign of underlying frustrations or a testing of boundaries. Understanding that back talk is a form of communication expressing a need or frustration, not just an act of defiance, can change how you respond to it, transforming potential conflicts into moments of learning and connection.

The first step in responding effectively is to maintain your calm. Reacting with similar frustration or anger will only escalate the situation. Instead, take a deep breath and give yourself a moment to collect your thoughts. Responding calmly and firmly sets a standard for respectful communication and shows that while their feelings are valid, disrespectful ways of expressing them are not. For instance, you might say, "I hear that you're upset, but we speak respectfully in our family. Can you tell me what's bothering you without using hurtful words?" This approach not only de-escalates the situation but also teaches your child that while their feelings are important, the way they express them matters as much.

Setting clear boundaries about respectful communication is crucial. It's important to communicate these expectations not in the heat of the moment but during calmer times, so your child knows what is expected before emotions flare. Discuss what respectful communication looks like and why it matters. Explain that it's about respecting each other's feelings and ensuring everyone feels heard and valued. When back talk does occur, remind them of these boundaries and the reasons behind them. If the disrespect continues, follow through with consistent consequences. These should be logical and related to the incident, such as losing the privilege to use their phone or spend time with friends for a period of time. Consistency is key in enforcing these boundaries; it helps children understand the seriousness of their behavior and the reliability of your responses.

Encouraging appropriate expression of feelings and opinions is another effective strategy. Teach your children how to express their thoughts and feelings constructively. Role-playing can be a helpful tool here. For example, if your child is upset about not being allowed to go out with friends, role-play the scenario where they express their disappointment respectfully, and you respond. Guide them on how to articulate their feelings clearly and calmly, using phrases like, "I feel upset because I was really looking forward to hanging out with my friends tonight." Encourage them to offer solutions or compromises, such as suggesting another day or a different activity that could be done together. This not only helps in the current situation but also equips them with skills to express themselves effectively in future interactions.

By understanding the reasons behind back talk, maintaining a calm and firm response, setting clear boundaries about respectful communication, and encouraging your child to express their feelings and opinions appropriately, you transform challenging interactions into opportunities for growth and learning. These strategies help manage backtalk and foster an environment where open and respectful dialogue is the norm, enhancing communication and understanding within your family.

7.7 Rebuilding After a Parental Meltdown: Steps to Recovery and Reconnection

As parents, we all have those moments when the pressures of daily life, the constant juggling of responsibilities, and our own emotional baggage collide spectacularly. It might be a shouted word, a hasty and unfair judgment, or an overreaction to a minor mishap—suddenly, you find yourself in the midst of a parental meltdown. Recognizing and acknowledging this meltdown is the first step toward healing. It's about admitting to yourself, and sometimes to your child, that you are not perfect. This admission isn't a sign of weakness; it demonstrates your humanity and is a critical lesson for your child in gracefully handling mistakes.

Apologizing to your child is crucial. It involves more than a simple "I'm sorry." It's about explaining what happened so they can understand without making excuses for your behavior. For instance, you might say, "I'm sorry for yelling. I got overwhelmed because I was trying to do many things simultaneously, and I didn't handle my feelings well. That wasn't fair to you." This kind of apology shows your child that everyone, even parents, can lose control sometimes, but taking responsibility for one's actions is what matters. It also teaches them about the nuances of human emotions and the importance of handling them responsibly.

Reflecting on what triggered your meltdown is another essential step. This reflection isn't just about identifying what went wrong but understanding the deeper reasons behind your reaction. Were you tired, stressed, or unwell? Were there unresolved issues from your day that you inadvertently took out on your family? Understanding these triggers helps you manage them better in the future. It might mean setting firmer boundaries around your time, learning more effective stress management techniques, or perhaps seeking professional help if the issues are deep-seated. This process of reflection is not only about preventing future meltdowns but also about personal growth and setting a healthy example for your children on how to handle personal challenges.

Rebuilding trust with your child involves consistent effort. After a meltdown, your child might feel wary or hurt. Reconnecting with them through quality time can help heal these wounds. Engage in activities that your child loves, be fully present during these moments, and show through your actions that you are still the loving, dependable parent they know. This might mean scheduling daily one-on-one time with your child, during which you can read together, play a game, or simply talk about how their day went. Let these moments be opportunities for you to demonstrate consistent emotional regulation, showing your child that you are working on managing your reactions better. This consistent effort not only mends the rifts caused by the meltdown but also strengthens your relationship in the long run, building a deeper bond based on understanding, respect, and mutual forgiveness.

Navigating the aftermath of a parental meltdown isn't easy, but it's a profoundly important process. It's about turning a moment of failure into a powerful lesson in emotional intelligence, responsibility, and resilience—both for you and your child. By acknowledging the meltdown, apologizing sincerely, reflecting on the triggers, and actively rebuilding trust, you not only recover from the incident but also enhance your role as a parent. You reinforce the values of accountability, learning, and unconditional love, ensuring that your family emerges stronger and more connected from the experience.

7.8 The Overwhelmed Parent: Strategies for Complex Family Dynamics

Imagine you're juggling three balls named work, parenting, and personal life, and suddenly, someone tosses a fourth ball called 'unexpected life event' into the mix. Feeling overwhelmed is like finding yourself catching more and more balls without the option to put any down. The signs of being overwhelmed aren't always as dramatic as a breakdown; they can be as subtle as a nagging fatigue, irritability over minor things, or a sense of disconnection from your family and friends. Recognizing these signs early is crucial in managing your emotional health. It's about noticing when you feel more tired than usual, when small tasks seem daunting, or when you snap at your kids for minor misbehaviors. These are signals that your emotional bandwidth is stretched thin, and it's time to implement strategies to regain balance and ensure you do not lose that vital connection with your family.

When the feeling of being overwhelmed starts creeping in, the first practical step is to prioritize your tasks. List down everything that you feel needs to be done, and then categorize these tasks into 'urgent,' 'important but not urgent,' and 'can wait.' Often, just writing down and organizing your tasks can provide a clearer perspective and reduce anxiety. Delegation is another crucial strategy. It's okay to ask for help, whether it's from family, friends, or professional services. It could be having a family member pick up the kids from school or hiring a temporary cleaner to manage household chores. Remember, asking for help is not a sign of weakness but a smart strategy to ensure you don't get overwhelmed.

During stressful times, maintaining emotional connections within your family is more important than ever. Ensure you set aside time daily to connect with your children and partner, if applicable. This could be something simple like sharing meals without the distraction of electronic devices or a bedtime routine where you talk about the day's highs and lows. These moments of connection act as anchors, maintaining the strength of your family bond even when the seas of life get rough.

Building resilience against overwhelm is not just about reacting to stress but also about proactively managing your well-being. Regular self-care is essential. This might mean setting aside time for activities that rejuvenate your spirit, like reading, yoga, or simply sitting quietly with a cup of tea. Community support plays a crucial role, too. Connecting with other parents in your local community or online can provide emotional support and practical advice. Sharing your experiences and hearing others' can normalize what you're going through and offer new insights or solutions.

By recognizing the signs of overwhelm early, prioritizing and delegating tasks, maintaining strong family connections, and building resilience through self-care and community support, you can manage the complexities of family dynamics more effectively. This approach helps ensure that despite the chaos that life sometimes throws our way, we can navigate through it without losing our sense of self or the closeness of our family ties.

7.9 When Parents Disagree: Finding Common Ground Through Self-Regulation

Navigating the choppy waters of parental disagreements can sometimes feel like you're steering a ship through a storm. Remember, it's natural for disagreements to arise, especially under the constant demands of parenting. However, how you handle these disagreements can strengthen your family unit or lead to further discord. The goal here is to foster an environment of respect, understanding, and cooperation, not just between you and your partner, but as a model for your children to handle conflicts constructively.

When disagreements occur, it's crucial to engage in respectful communication. This means listening actively to your partner without interrupting, validating their feelings even if you disagree, and expressing your own views without blame or criticism. Start discussions with "I feel" statements rather than "you" statements, which can feel accusatory. For instance, say, "I feel overwhelmed when I have to handle bedtime routines alone," instead of "You never help with the kids at night." This approach opens up a dialogue that focuses on solving problems together rather than assigning blame.

Self-regulation plays a pivotal role in managing conflicts. It's about being able to hold back on immediate reactionary impulses and understanding that taking a moment to cool down can significantly change the course of a conversation. If a discussion starts to heat up, it's okay to say, "I think I need a few minutes to cool down." Taking this time isn't avoiding the problem but preparing yourself to address it more thoughtfully. Use these moments to assess what's really behind your feelings. Are you actually upset about the dishes, or is it more about feeling unappreciated? Reenter the discussion with a clearer mind and possibly a new perspective that can lead to more productive outcomes.

Creating a detailed parenting plan together can also help in reducing conflicts. This plan should cover various scenarios, from daily routines to how you'll handle discipline, ensuring you both know what to expect and have agreed to it in advance. This clarity can prevent many spur-of-the-moment disagreements and makes co-parenting a more seamless process. Sit down together and discuss each aspect of parenting, from who does pick-ups and drop-offs to how you'll manage screen time. Write down your decisions and revisit the plan periodically to make adjustments as needed, keeping the lines of communication always open.

Sometimes, despite your best efforts, you might find yourselves stuck in a loop of ongoing disagreements. In such cases, seeking outside support from a mediator or counselor can be beneficial. These professionals can provide neutral ground and experienced insights into resolving conflicts. They can help you explore underlying issues influencing your interactions and guide you toward resolving them constructively. Remember, seeking help is not a testament to failure but a proactive step towards preserving and strengthening your family's harmony.

By embracing respectful communication, self-regulation, creating a shared parenting plan, and seeking help when needed, you can navigate parental disagreements with maturity and compassion. These approaches resolve conflicts and teach your children invaluable lessons about love, respect, and teamwork in relationships.

As we close this chapter on navigating specific challenges with self-regulation, we reflect on the diverse scenarios that test our patience, wisdom, and emotional flexibility. Each section, from managing public tantrums to handling bedtime routines, emphasizes the profound impact of self-regulation, not just on our children but on the overall health of our family dynamics. As we move forward, let these insights guide you in fostering a home environment where challenges are met with resilience, understanding, and cooperative spirit, setting the stage for a seamless transition into our following discussions on how taking care of yourself is essential in this journey.

Chapter Eight

Self-Care for Parents

Imagine it's one of those days where everything seems to be happening simultaneously. You've dropped your kids at school, rushed to work, managed back-to-back meetings, and now you're on dinner duty, all while balancing the ever-growing pile of laundry that seems to have a life of its own. In the whirlwind of such days, pausing might seem like a luxury you can't afford. But here's the truth—taking that pause, that moment for yourself, isn't just a luxury; it's a necessity. Self-care is the anchor that keeps you grounded in the stormy seas of parenting, providing you with the relief and empowerment you need to navigate through it all.

8.1 Self-Care Isn't Selfish: Recharging for Resilience

Self-Care Definition

Often, self-care is pictured as a long, leisurely day at the spa or an indulgent shopping spree. While these can be delightful breaks, everyday self-care is much more accessible and essential. It's about taking intentional actions to care for your physical, mental, and emotional health. This isn't selfish; it's a critical practice that enables you to be the parent you aspire to be. When you're well-rested, emotionally balanced, and physically healthy, you're better equipped to meet the demands of parenting with patience and empathy. Think of self-care as putting on your oxygen mask first before assisting others; it's about ensuring you're at your best to be fully present and engaged for your children.

Assessing Personal Needs

Every parent's self-care needs are unique. They fluctuate based on what's happening in your life, the ages of your children, your work demands, and your personal health. Start by taking a moment to assess your current stressors. Are you getting enough sleep? Do you feel constantly overwhelmed by your to-do list? Are you taking any time to pursue activities that you enjoy or that relax you? Answering these questions can help you identify the areas where you need to focus your self-care efforts. Remember, self-care isn't a one-size-fits-all solution; it's a personal recipe you need to tailor to your tastes and needs.

Simple Self-Care Practices

Integrating self-care into your busy schedule might seem daunting, but there are simple practices you can adopt that only require a little time or preparation. For instance, spending just five minutes each morning sitting quietly with a cup of coffee before the kids wake up can set a calm tone for the day. Or, try a ten-minute walk during lunch to clear your mind and stretch your legs. Even taking deep, deliberate breaths for a few minutes can significantly reduce stress levels. When done consistently, these small practices can substantially impact your overall well-being.

The Impact of Self-Care

The benefits of regular self-care extend beyond your well-being—they positively affect your whole family. Taking care of yourself makes you happier, more patient, and more responsive. This creates a more positive home environment and models healthy habits for your children. Plus, when you're less stressed, you can make more thoughtful decisions and respond more calmly to parenting challenges.

Setting Self-Care Goals

Setting specific achievable goals can help make self-care a regular part of your routine. These could be as simple as deciding to read for pleasure for 15 minutes before bed each night or scheduling a weekly coffee date with a friend. Write down these goals, and think about how to realistically incorporate them into your schedule. Having clear, defined goals makes you more likely to commit to them.

Self-Care Planning

To effectively integrate self-care into your life, plan it like any other important activity. Use a planner or digital calendar to block out time for your self-care activities, treating them with the same importance as a business meeting or a parent-teacher conference. Planning ahead also helps manage expectations with your family, allowing you to communicate when you'll be taking time for yourself and why it's important. This not only helps you commit to your self-care routine but also sets a healthy boundary that your family can respect and support.

Incorporating self-care into your daily life doesn't have to be overwhelming or time-consuming. By defining what self-care means to you, assessing your needs, setting realistic goals, and planning effectively, you can enhance your well-being without turning your schedule upside down. Remember, taking care of yourself isn't just about personal health—it's about setting the foundation for a happy, healthy family.

8.2 Building Your Support Circle: The Role of Community in Parental Well-being

Parenting, while fulfilling, can sometimes feel like an island—especially on days filled with unexpected challenges and little victories that only fellow parents might genuinely understand. That's where your community steps in, not just as a network but as a lifeline of shared experiences and mutual support. Building a community around your parenting journey is invaluable. It enriches your life with camaraderie and understanding. It strengthens your resilience as you navigate the ups and downs of raising children.

Let's explore how to weave these crucial connections into your life. The beauty of today's interconnected world is that it offers numerous avenues for meeting like-minded parents. Start locally. Look for parent groups in your neighborhood. These might be formally organized through local community centers, churches, or schools or informally arranged on community bulletin boards or in local parks. Attending local events, school meetings, or children's sports activities can also be a great way to meet other parents. These face-to-face interactions create strong bonds and provide a platform for sharing resources, from babysitting co-ops to clothing exchanges, which can be immensely helpful.

Online forums and social media groups offer another layer of connectivity, especially if you're looking for advice or companionship during those late-night feedings or early-morning wake-ups. Platforms like Facebook, Reddit, and specialized parenting websites host myriad parent groups where you can find others dealing with similar issues, whether toddler tantrums or navigating teen social dynamics. These spaces can be particularly beneficial for single parents, parents of children with special needs, or those living in remote areas where in-person gatherings are less accessible, providing a virtual support network at your fingertips.

Asking for help is a skill that every parent needs to hone for their well-being and that of their family. It's normal to feel hesitant about reaching out but remember, every parent has been in a spot where a little support could make a big difference. Start small. It could be as simple as asking a neighbor to watch your child for an hour so you can run an errand or asking a friend to share meal prep tips. Gradually, you may find it easier to ask for more considerable support, like coordinating carpools or arranging childcare swaps. Each act of asking builds your community support network and sets an example of healthy interdependence for your children.

Creating supportive spaces is essential. These should be environments where openness and non-judgmental dialogue are the norms. Establish ground rules that foster respect and confidentiality, whether it's a coffee meet-up or an online chat session. In these spaces, allow yourself and others to share successes and setbacks without fear of criticism. Celebrate the milestones, empathize with the challenges, and share the laughter and tears. These moments of shared vulnerability are powerful; they deepen connections and remind everyone in the group that no one has to parent alone.

Cultivating these relationships and networks takes time and effort, but the rewards are manifold. They provide emotional support, practical help, and the kind of understanding that only those on similar paths can offer. As you build and nurture these connections, you'll likely find that your parenting experience is richer and more enjoyable. Remember, in the vast community of parents worldwide, your experiences are unique, yet the emotional journey of parenting is universal. By reaching out, you tap into a wellspring of collective wisdom and compassion, making your parenting journey a bit easier and more connected.

8.3 The Importance of Hobbies and Personal Time in Parental Self-Regulation

When you think about hobbies, what comes to mind? Maybe it's painting landscapes, tinkering with technology, gardening, or perhaps playing guitar. Hobbies and personal interests are more than just activities to fill your spare time; they are vital outlets for creativity, stress relief, and personal expression. In the whirlwind of parenting duties, it's easy to forget that you are also an individual with passions and interests that don't necessarily revolve around your role as a parent. Engaging in hobbies can be a fantastic release from the pressures of parenting, providing not just a sense of accomplishment but also enhancing your emotional well-being by keeping you connected to your unique self.

Finding time for these personal activities might seem nearly impossible with a packed parenting schedule. However, integrating personal time into your life doesn't require grand gestures; it's about carving out small niches of time throughout your week. Start by looking at your weekly schedule with a critical eye—can any tasks be batched together to free up an hour here or there? Perhaps waking up earlier while the house is still quiet could be your golden hour for writing or yoga. Or maybe you can use the time during your child's dance class or soccer practice to sketch, read, or engage in any portable hobby. It's about seeing time not just as slots to be filled with tasks but as opportunities for personal growth and relaxation.

Sharing interests with your children can also be a rewarding way to nurture your passions while strengthening your bond with them. It's a chance to let them see another side of you, apart from being a parent. If you love gardening, involve them in planting seeds or watering plants. If you're an avid reader, set aside time for a family reading hour where everyone picks a book and shares something about their reading. Not only does this teach children the value of personal time and interests, but it also allows them to see the joy these activities bring you, which can inspire them to pursue their own interests.

However, balancing personal time with family time can indeed be challenging. It often feels like there isn't enough time to meet everyone's needs and reserve some for yourself. The key here is to remember that quality trumps quantity. It's not about how many hours you spend together but how meaningful those hours are. Communicate openly with your family about why personal time is essential to you and how it makes you a happier, more fulfilled individual and, consequently, a better parent. Encourage everyone in the family to identify and pursue their interests and respect each other's need for time to engage in these activities. This mutual respect for personal time can lead to a healthier family dynamic where everyone's needs for personal development and family time are balanced.

In weaving these threads of individual pursuits into the fabric of family life, you enrich not only your own life but also set a profound example for your children about the importance of maintaining individuality and personal well-being even within the demands of family responsibilities. This balance is crucial not just for personal satisfaction but also for modeling healthy lifestyle choices that emphasize the importance of taking care of one's mental and emotional health through enjoyable and fulfilling activities.

8.4 Self-Care on a Budget: Affordable Ways to Recharge

In the bustling life of parenting, finding time and resources for self-care can sometimes feel like a luxury reserved for those with spare time and disposable income. However, the essence of self-care is rooted in simplicity and creativity, not in how much you spend. It's about carving out moments for yourself that rejuvenate your spirit without breaking the bank. Let's explore how you can infuse your life with affordable self-care practices that are as nurturing as they are budget-friendly.

Creativity is your greatest ally when it comes to self-care on a budget. Think outside the traditional spa day or retail therapy. Self-care can be as simple as a quiet morning with a book from the library, a homemade spa treatment using ingredients from your kitchen, or a creative craft project that reuses materials you already have at home. These activities not only save money but also foster a sense of accomplishment and personal expression. You can craft a stress-relieving journal from old notebooks or create a soothing bath soak with common household items like oatmeal and dried lavender. Each creative act of self-care is a reminder that the value lies not in how much you spend but in the intention behind the action.

Utilizing free resources is another effective way to engage in self-care. Many communities offer free or low-cost classes that can enhance your well-being. Look for yoga sessions in the park, community art classes, or workshops at local libraries. These activities provide a dual benefit: they offer a chance to relax and learn new skills while connecting you with your community, which can be a self-care boost.

Online resources also abound, offering everything from free meditation apps to fitness videos that can guide you through a home workout. These tools make it easy to fit self-care into your daily routine, whether you have five minutes or an hour to spare.

The beauty of self-care lies in the simple pleasures that enrich your life, and many of these cost nothing at all. Consider the restorative power of nature: a walk in the local park, an afternoon spent gardening, or simply sitting under a tree can be profoundly calming and rejuvenating. These moments allow you to disconnect from the demands of daily life and reconnect with the natural world, which is a potent form of mental and emotional refreshment. Likewise, engaging in mindfulness practices like deep breathing or mindful observation doesn't cost a dime. Still, it offers significant benefits in stress reduction and increased mental clarity.

Shifting your mindset about what constitutes self-care is crucial. It's easy to think of self-care as requiring spare time and money. Still, when you view it as essential to your well-being, you start to recognize the many opportunities each day offers to care for yourself. This shift in perspective encourages you to make self-care an integral part of your life rather than something that happens outside of it. It's about weaving small, restorative practices into the fabric of your daily routine, turning ordinary moments into opportunities for self-nourishment and reflection.

Embracing creativity, utilizing free resources, enjoying simple pleasures, and shifting your mindset about self-care are all ways to ensure that taking care of yourself is accessible, affordable, and a natural part of your life.

8.5 Nutrition and Sleep: The Foundations of Emotional Stability

When you think about the building blocks of a stable and happy household, nutrition and sleep might not be the first things that come to mind. Still, they are foundational to maintaining emotional balance and overall health in your family. It's fascinating how much what we eat and how well we sleep can influence our moods, energy levels, and even our interactions with each other. Let's unpack the significant roles that nutrition and sleep play in our lives and explore practical ways to enhance these areas, ensuring you and your children can thrive.

Nutrition's Role

The connection between what we eat and how we feel is profound. Nutritious foods that are rich in vitamins, minerals, and other essential nutrients contribute to the functioning of our brains and bodies. For example, omega-3 fatty acids found in fish like salmon enhance brain health, which can improve mood and cognitive function. Similarly, foods high in fiber, such as fruits, vegetables, and whole grains, can help stabilize blood sugar levels, which in turn can prevent mood swings and irritability. To incorporate these benefits into your family's diet, start by introducing various healthy foods at meals. Make it a fun and collaborative activity with your kids by involving them in meal planning and preparation. This helps educate them about nutritious choices and makes them more likely to try new foods. Additionally, try to minimize the intake of processed foods and sugars, which can cause energy spikes and crashes, affecting mood and behavior.

Sleep Hygiene

For parents, good sleep hygiene might seem like a distant dream, especially with young kids in the house. However, prioritizing sleep is crucial for emotional and physical health. Lack of sleep can lead to a short temper, difficulty concentrating, and a general feeling of being overwhelmed—all of which can make parenting even more challenging. To improve sleep quality, establish a regular sleep schedule and stick to it as much as possible, even on weekends. Create a bedtime routine that signals to your body it's time to wind down; this might include reading a book, taking a warm bath, or doing some gentle stretches. Make your bedroom a sleep sanctuary: keep it cool, dark, and quiet, and invest in a comfortable mattress and pillows.

Modeling Healthy Habits

Children learn by example, so it's vital that they see you practicing good nutrition and sleep habits. Share meals as a family as often as you can, and use this time to show your kids that eating healthily is not just good for the body; it's also enjoyable. Discuss the benefits of the foods you eat, and encourage your kids to listen to their bodies to recognize when they're hungry or full. Similarly, by adhering to a consistent bedtime routine yourself, you show your children that sleep is a priority. Share with them how good sleep improves your mood and energy, helping them understand why developing good sleep habits is essential from a young age.

Practical Changes

To make lasting improvements in nutrition and sleep, small, practical changes can be incredibly effective. For nutrition, consider planning your meals for the week ahead. This can help ensure you have all the ingredients for healthy meals, reducing the temptation to order takeout on busy days. You might also set a goal to introduce one new fruit or vegetable each week to expand your family's palate. For sleep, evaluate your family's evening activities. If your schedule is too hectic, it might be worth cutting back on evening commitments to allow everyone more downtime before bed. Encourage activities that help wind down, like puzzles or reading, instead of stimulating ones like video games.

By focusing on nutrition and sleep, you're taking essential steps to enhance your family's emotional stability and overall well-being. These foundational aspects of health play a critical role in how you and your children experience and interact with the world. With some thoughtful adjustments and a commitment to these areas, you can foster a nurturing environment that supports both physical health and emotional resilience, paving the way for more harmonious family dynamics and happier, healthier lives.

To assist in remembering key elements

Recognize your needs

Engage in hobbies

Seek support

Take care of your body

This chapter offers a comprehensive guide to nurturing your well-being as you navigate the complex terrain of raising children. By embracing self-care as non-negotiable, forging connections within communities, indulging personal passions within budgetary constraints, and prioritizing nutrition and sleep, you not only enhance your resilience but also create a nurturing environment where your family can thrive.

Next, we will explore essential actions aimed at fostering sustainable self-regulation practices within your own life and that of your family, facilitating their ongoing development and flourishing.

Chapter Nine

Sustaining Growth and Embracing Change

I magine you're painting a room in your home. You've chosen a vibrant color, prepped the walls, and started with enthusiasm. But as you progress, you notice missed spots, streaks that need smoothing out, and areas that require a touch-up. Parenting, much like painting, is a continuous process of growth and refinement. It's about setting goals, incorporating feedback, adjusting plans, and celebrating the progress—no matter how small. This ongoing cycle helps you and your family evolve together, fostering harmony and emotional growth despite the challenges.

9.1 Setting Goals for Emotional Growth and Family Harmony

Goal-Setting Framework

Setting goals for emotional growth and family harmony starts with understanding what you aim to achieve and why it's important. For instance, perhaps you want to enhance communication within your family, manage conflicts more effectively, or foster a deeper connection with your children. Each goal needs to be specific, measurable, achievable, relevant, and time-bound (SMART). This framework not only provides clarity but also makes the process of achieving these goals more tangible and less daunting.

Steps for each goal

- Step 1: Choose and write your first primary goal.

- Step 2: Decide when you want your goal to be achieved. Use formulations like "by the end of the week," "within a month," etc. Adding a specific date can be helpful, especially for longer durations, to avoid having to count the days each time you refer to your goal.

- Step 3: Write 2 or more sub-goals that are actionable and measurable steps. Be specific and use quantifiable terms such as "every day," "at least once a day," "more than X times per week," "at every meal," etc.

Example:

- <u>Main goal</u>: Dedicate more time to Self-Care by the end of the month.

- <u>Sub-goals</u>:

1. Meditate at least 3 times per week.

2. Take 1 relaxing bath per week.

3. Take a 10-minute walk every day.

Make these goals visible—write them down and place them where everyone can see them, like on the refrigerator or a family bulletin board. This visibility keeps the goals in everyone's mind and serves as a constant reminder of what you are all working toward together. You can write as many sub-goals as you want to help you create concrete steps and ideas to achieve your goals. These sub-goals, along with the tiny steps and efforts toward them, are the elements you will track.

The workbook contains additional ideas, templates, and examples for guidance. Feel free to refer to it as a guideline.

Visual Element: Goal-Tracking Chart

To visually track your family's progress, consider creating a goal-tracking chart. This can be a simple board or digital spreadsheet where each family member can update their progress toward the goals. Utilize stickers or another visual marker as a step-tracking tool to monitor progress. This visual element helps keep everyone accountable and provides a clear picture of how far you've come and what needs to be focused on, enhancing the overall process of growth and adjustment in your family dynamics. There's no strict rule here; simply place a sticker near the relevant goal each time you take a step and exert significant effort to attain it. When the deadline for your goal approaches, reassess it and determine if the goal has been achieved or if adjustments are necessary. If you find your goal accomplished (especially when consistently achieving sub-goals), mark it as done and celebrate (more details in a few pages).

Incorporating Feedback

Feedback is crucial in goal setting, especially when it concerns family dynamics. It is essential to create a safe space where each family member can express their thoughts and feelings about the goals and progress. Regular family meetings can be an effective platform for this exchange. During these meetings, encourage everyone to share their perspectives on what's working and what isn't, and what they feel might need more focus. This feedback is invaluable as it provides insights to help refine and adjust your strategies, ensuring the goals remain relevant and aligned with everyone's needs.

For younger children who might not articulate their thoughts as clearly, consider using creative methods like drawing or storytelling to help them express how they feel about the family's progress. This makes the process engaging for them and enables you to gather accurate feedback to guide further adjustments.

Adjusting Goals

Flexibility is key in the journey of emotional growth and family harmony. As your family evolves and external circumstances change, your goals might need to be adjusted to align with your current needs and realities. This adjustment process should be a collaborative effort, considering the feedback from all family members.

For example, if a goal was initially set to have family dinners together five nights a week, but extracurricular activities or work schedules make this impractical, consider adjusting the goal to three nights a week. Alternatively, you could re-define the goal to focus on quality rather than quantity, ensuring that the time spent together during those dinners is fully engaged and free from distractions like electronic devices.

9.2 Celebrating Progress: Recognizing and Rewarding Your Growth

Following our discussion on goal setting, this section emphasizes the importance of acknowledging and celebrating small victories and efforts—like maintaining composure during a child's public tantrum or successfully transitioning your toddler to sleeping through the night. These seemingly minor successes are pivotal to your development as a mindful parent, reinforcing the positive strides you're making and underscoring that all progress, regardless of size, is valuable.

Visualize your parenting journey as a garden where daily actions and decisions plant seeds of patience, understanding, and love. Celebrating small wins acts as a moment to observe the budding sprouts and flowers, a testament to your efforts' fruition. This recognition boosts morale and motivates continued care for your garden, especially through challenging times. For instance, congratulating yourself for a day spent without raising your voice, by sharing the achievement with a partner or noting it in a journal, serves as a potent reminder of your growth.

Equally critical is rewarding these efforts. Rewards, which need not be materialistic, reinforce positive behaviors. They could range from extra bedtime stories, special outings, to enjoying a hobby or guilt-free relaxation. The essence lies in selecting meaningful and enjoyable rewards and reinforcing positive behaviors. For example, praising your child for consistently using manners with a special sticker or verbal affirmation can be incredibly motivating. Engaging in reflective practice is another key element in celebrating growth. Regular reflection—through journaling, meditation, or family meetings—offers a wider perspective on the changes occurring over time. This practice allows you to pause and review your challenges, how you've addressed them, and the progress you've achieved, often unveiling growth that daily life's hustle may obscure.

The significance of recognizing and celebrating progress on self-esteem and family morale is profound. When children see their efforts acknowledged, it boosts their confidence and reinforces their self-worth, teaching them the impact of their actions. This lesson also extends to parents; celebrating small victories reminds you of your strengths and capabilities, enhancing self-esteem and morale. Thus, recognizing and rewarding growth is not merely about marking achievements but about laying a foundation of confidence and resilience that supports your family through life's challenges, cultivating a culture that values progress and views every challenge as a learning opportunity.

9.3 Embracing Change: When to Adapt Your Self-Regulation Strategies

Change is as inevitable in parenting as it is in life. Just when you think you've mastered your toddler's routines, they morph into preschoolers with entirely different needs and behaviors. Or perhaps you find that techniques that once eased your teenager's anxieties no longer have the same effect. Recognizing when it's time to adapt your self-regulation strategies is crucial for addressing immediate challenges and fostering an environment where every family member can thrive.

Let's talk about the signals that suggest a need for change. These signs often manifest as recurring conflicts, such as continuous disagreements over homework or bedtime routines that no longer go smoothly. Another red flag could be a noticeable plateau or decline in the emotional growth of your family dynamics. Perhaps you've noticed increased tension or less open communication within your family circle. These situations are indicators that your current methods need revisiting. It's much like when a gardener notices that despite adequate water and sunlight, a plant fails to thrive because the soil needs replenishment or the plant has outgrown its current pot.

Adopting a flexible approach to self-regulation is essential. Life throws curveballs, and what worked yesterday might not work tomorrow. This flexibility might mean adjusting your expectations or trying new strategies that better align with your family's evolving needs. For instance, as children grow, they require different levels of autonomy and guidance. An approach that involves strict supervision may need to shift towards one that fosters independent decision-making to better support an adolescent's development.

Furthermore, embracing a flexible mindset encourages resilience in you and models this adaptability for your children. It teaches them that change is a part of life and that adjusting our strategies and expectations is a natural response to new circumstances. This life lesson is invaluable, as it equips them with the mindset to face their own challenges and changes constructively throughout their lives.

Including your family in discussions about changing strategies is another vital aspect. When family members are invited to express their views and contribute ideas, they are more likely to understand and support the changes. This collaborative approach strengthens the family bond and enhances the effectiveness of new strategies. For example, suppose you decide to implement a new rule about screen time. Discussing this change with your children, understanding their perspectives, and possibly adjusting the rule based on their feedback can lead to smoother implementation and greater adherence.

Continuous learning and openness to new techniques play a significant role in successfully adapting your self-regulation strategies. The world of parenting advice is vast and continually evolving. New research might offer insights that could be game-changing for your family dynamics. Staying informed about the latest parenting strategies through books, workshops, or online courses can give you a broader toolkit. It's akin to a chef who continually learns new techniques and recipes; the more you know, the more effectively you can respond to your family's unique needs.

Moreover, being open to learning also sets a powerful example for your children about the value of lifelong learning and adaptability. It shows them that being open to learning and changing is not just necessary but a positive approach to living a fuller, more responsive life.

As you move forward, remember that adapting your strategies isn't a sign of previous failures but a proactive approach to meeting your family's changing needs. It's about making adjustments that align with your family's growth and continuing to provide a supportive, nurturing environment where every member can flourish. So, take a moment to reflect on the dynamics of your family. Are there signs suggesting it's time for a change? How can you be more flexible, and what new strategies might you explore? Engaging with these questions is the first step in a continuous cycle of growth and adaptation—an ongoing process that enriches both your journey as a parent and the lives of your children.

9.4 The Journey Ahead: Continuing Your Path to Mindful Parenting

As parents, we all aim to create a loving, nurturing environment where our children can grow and thrive. But like any significant endeavor, the path to mindful parenting isn't always smooth. It requires a long-term commitment and a perspective that views each day as a step towards growth, even when those steps feel more like stumbles. Embracing this outlook transforms challenges from stumbling blocks into stepping stones, opportunities to deepen our understanding and refine our approaches.

When you view parenting through this long-term lens, you begin to see the importance of resilience—not just as a trait to cultivate in your children but as a crucial aspect of your parenting practice. It's about staying committed to the practices of self-regulation and mindful parenting, even when the immediate results aren't as visible as you might hope. One day, your toddler's tantrum might leave you feeling defeated, but rather than seeing this as a setback, it can be an opportunity to practice patience and reflect on different strategies that might work better next time.

Commitment to mindfulness in parenting means consistently applying the principles you've learned, even when tiredness clouds your judgment or when external pressures mount. It involves setting aside time for regular reflection on what's working and what isn't and gently reminding yourself why you chose this path. Keeping a journal can be a helpful tool in this regard, providing a space to record thoughts, feelings, and reactions on difficult days as well as the good ones, helping you to maintain a balanced perspective.

Another essential element in sustaining your path is your support network. This network, whether it consists of family, friends, or a more formal support group, is invaluable. These people can offer a listening ear, a word of encouragement, or a different perspective when you're too close to a problem to see it clearly. They're also there to celebrate with you when you overcome challenges or reach new milestones in your parenting. Maintaining and seeking out these connections not only supports your emotional well-being but also reinforces your commitment to mindful parenting by surrounding you with others who share or support your values and goals.

Let's also consider the powerful role of envisioning the future. Imagine a family life where the principles of mindful parenting and self-regulation have become as natural as breathing. Where open communication, emotional resilience, and mutual respect are the norms rather than the exceptions. Holding this vision in your mind can be incredibly motivating. It's a reminder of what you're working towards—a healthier, more harmonious family life—and can reinvigorate your commitment to the practices that will help you get there. This vision isn't just a dream; it's a potential reality that you have the power to create through your daily choices and actions.

As you continue on this path, remember that every day won't be perfect, and that's okay. Mindful parenting is not about perfection but about progress. It's about making more conscious choices, becoming more connected with your children, and responding to family challenges with thoughtfulness rather than reactivity. This approach doesn't eliminate difficulties, but it does change how you handle them, making the family journey smoother and more enjoyable for everyone involved.

In closing this chapter, remember that the journey of mindful parenting is ongoing. Each day offers a new opportunity to apply the principles of self-regulation, to learn from your experiences, and to grow alongside your children. Keep your long-term vision in mind, stay committed to your practices, lean on your support network, and continue to learn and adapt. These efforts will not only enhance your family life in the present but will also lay the groundwork for a future where mindful parenting is an integral part of your family's culture.

Keeping the Calm Alive

Now, you have everything you need to create a more peaceful and connected family life, and it's time to pass on your newfound knowledge and show other parents where they can find the same help.

Simply by leaving your honest opinion of this book on Amazon, you'll show other parents where they can find the information they're looking for, and pass their passion for emotional balance and family harmony forward.

Thank you for being so helpful. The journey to self-regulation and mindful parenting are kept alive when we pass on our knowledge – and you're helping me to do just that.

>>> Click here to leave your review on Amazon

Conclusion

As we wrap up our journey together through the pages of this book, I want to reflect on the incredible path we've navigated. From our first steps in understanding the pivotal role of self-regulation in parenting, through uncovering our personal and external triggers, to embracing practical strategies and exercises that enhance our family dynamics—what a journey it has been!

We've delved deep into the importance of self-awareness and how it fosters emotional intelligence. We've explored the transformative power of modeling self-regulation for our children and how our actions can teach them to manage their emotions effectively. Together, we've tackled practical strategies for managing stress and triggers and seen how vital communication is in building and strengthening our family relationships.

I invite you now to pause and reflect on your own personal growth throughout this journey. Take a moment to acknowledge the significant shifts in your perspective and behavior, the enlightening moments of insight, and the courageous steps you've taken toward becoming a more mindful parent. These changes are not just profound, they are a testament to your dedication and resilience, and they are creating a positive ripple effect within your home.

Self-regulation is not just a personal tool; it's a family revolution. It brings harmony, understanding, and deeper connections to our relationships, transforming our homes into sanctuaries of peace and empathy. Remember, the practice of self-regulation and the exercises we've explored are not a 'one and done'—they are part of an ongoing, exciting journey of learning, growth, and adaptation.

I encourage you to keep the momentum going. Continue to practice the strategies we've shared, and keep the lines of communication open with your children. Establish routines that support emotional regulation and make mindfulness a daily practice. Each small step is a building block in creating a stable and loving environment.

For those who wish to delve even deeper and have an easily accessible guide at their fingertips, consider picking up the workbook that accompanies this book. It's designed to provide structured exercises and insights to further reinforce your learning and practice.

I also invite you to share your stories and progress. Connect with others on the same journey and celebrate each other's successes. Your experiences can inspire and uplift others, and in turn, their stories can provide you with encouragement and new ideas.

In closing, I leave you with a message of hope and empowerment. The journey of self-regulation and mindful parenting is challenging but filled with opportunities for growth and joy. Each one of us has the power to make profound changes in our family life. Through dedication, patience, and love, we can transform our family dynamics and create a legacy of emotional intelligence and resilience for our children.

Thank you for allowing me to be a part of your journey. Here's to continuing our path toward a more mindful, compassionate, and connected parenting experience. Together, let's keep striving towards a family life filled with peace, understanding, and love.

References

1. Ackerman, C. E. (2021, April 29). Emotional regulation: 6 key skills to regulate emotions. Positive Psychology. https://positivepsychology.com/emotion-regulation/

2. Ackerman, C. E. (2021, April 29). What is self-regulation? (+95 skills and strategies). Positive Psychology. https://positivepsychology.com/self-regulation/

3. Alliance Health Equity. (2021, July 30). Why getting organized is good for your mental health. Alliance Health Equity. https://alliancehealthequity.org/why-getting-organized-is-good-for-your-mental-health/

4. American Academy of Pediatrics. (2008). Effective discipline for children. Pediatrics, 121(4), e1001-e1007. https://www.ncbi.nlm.nih.gov/pmc/articles/PMC2719514/

5. American Psychological Association. (n.d.). Strategies for controlling your anger: Keeping anger in check. American Psychological Association. https://www.apa.org/topics/anger/strategies-controlling

6. APA. (2002). Family routines and rituals may improve relationships and health, experts say. American Psychological Association. https://www.apa.org/news/press/releases/2002/12/rituals

7. Bradley, R. H., & Corwyn, R. F. (2002). Recognition for positive behavior as a critical youth development strategy. Journal of Youth and Adolescence, 31(5), 341-355. https://www.ncbi.nlm.nih.gov/pmc/articles/PMC3361320/

8. Brody, J. (2018, September 25). Practicing mindfulness benefits parents and children, UW study says. UW News. https://www.washington.edu/news/2018/09/25/practicing-mindfulness-benefits-parents-and-children-uw-study-says/

9. Brody, J. (2018, September 25). Practicing mindfulness benefits parents and children, UW study says. UW News. https://www.washington.edu/news/2018/09/25/practicing-mindfulness-benefits-parents-and-children-uw-study-says/

10. Child Mind Institute. (n.d.). Angry kids: Dealing with explosive behavior. Child Mind Institute. https://childmind.org/article/angry-kids-dealing-with-explosive-behavior/

11. Child Mind Institute. (2021, April 20). Practice mindful parenting: Mindfulness techniques. Child Mind Institute. https://childmind.org/article/mindful-parenting-2/

12. Colorado State University Extension. (2019, August 15). 10 tips for successful family meetings. Colorado State University Extension. https://extension.colostate.edu/topic-areas/family-home-consumer/10-tips-for-successful-family-meetings/

13. Duncan, L. G., Coatsworth, J. D., & Greenberg, M. T. (2009). A model of mindful parenting: Implications for parent-child relationships and prevention research. Clinical Child and Family Psychology Review, 12(3), 255-270. https://www.ncbi.nlm.nih.gov/pmc/articles/PMC2730447/

14. Emotional Intelligence Magazine. (2021, January 13). Why self-awareness is essential for a healthy parent-child relationship. Emotional Intelligence Magazine. https://www.ei-magazine.com/post/why-self-awareness-is-essential-for-a-healthy-parent-child-relationship

15. Eisenberg, N., & Eggum, N. D. (2009). The role of empathy and compassion in conflict resolution. Social and Personality Psychology Compass, 3(3), 368-383. https://journals.sagepub.com/doi/10.1177/1754073919838609

16. Felitti, V. J., Anda, R. F., & Nordenberg, D. (1998). Adverse childhood experiences and their relation to adult health outcomes. American Journal of Preventive Medicine, 14(4), 245-258. https://www.ncbi.nlm.nih.gov/pmc/articles/PMC6447511/

17. Gross, J. J. (2014). Environmental strategies of affect regulation and their effects on emotion and social behavior. Annual Review of Psychology, 65, 37-68. https://www.ncbi.nlm.nih.gov/pmc/articles/PMC5915835/

18. Gottman, J. M. (2019, October 23). How to strengthen your child's emotional intelligence. The Gottman Institute. https://www.gottman.com/blog/strengthen-childs-emotional-intelligence/

19. Harvard Graduate School of Education. (n.d.). Positive self-talk and problem-solving. Making Caring Common Project. https://mcc.gse.harvard.edu/resources-for-families/positive-self-talk

20. Honor Your Emotions. (2021, April 22). The 5 benefits of parent counseling. Honor Your Emotions. https://honoryouremotions.com/the-5-benefits-of-parent-counsel

21. Jai Institute for Parenting. (n.d.). What is emotional self-regulation in parenting? Jai Institute for Parenting. https://www.jaiinstituteforparenting.com/what-is-emotional-self-regulation-in-parenting

22. Johnson, J., & Paredes, Y. (2021). Parent emotional regulation: A meta-analytic review of its association with parenting outcomes. Journal of Early Adolescence, 41(1), 45-58. http://journals.sagepub.com/doi/10.1177/01650254211051086

23. Lewis, A. (2022, March 14). How parental stress can affect a child's health. Psychology Today. https://www.psychologytoday.com/us/blog/the-baby-scientist/202203/how-parental-stress-can-affect-childs-health

24. Merrick, M. T., & Ford, D. C. (2018). A systematic review of parental burnout and related factors. BMC Public Health, 18, 1782. https://bmcpubl ichealth.biomedcentral.com/articles/10.1186/s12889-024-17829-y

25. Mindful Schools. (2020, October 5). Four principles for mindful communi- cation with kids. Mindful Schools. https://www.mindfulschools.org/personal -practice/four-principles-of-mindful-communication-with-kids/

26. Morin, A. (2020, October 28). Examples of positive discipline techniques. Verywell Family. https://www.verywellfamily.com/examples-of-positive-discipli ne-1095049

27. Murray, D. W., Rosanbalm, K., & Christopoulos, C. (2015). Co-reg- ulation from birth through young adulthood: A practice brief. Frank Porter Graham Child Development Institute, University of North Caroli- na. https://fpg.unc.edu/sites/fpg.unc.edu/files/resources/reports-and-policy-b riefs/Co-RegulationFromBirthThroughYoungAdulthood.pdf

28. Nunez, J. C., & Martin-Albo, J. (2010). Emotional intelligence and mental health in the family. Journal of Adolescence, 33(5), 771-780. https://www.ncb i.nlm.nih.gov/pmc/articles/PMC7503667/

29. Psy-Ed. (2019, June 17). A guide to setting age-appropriate limits for children. Psy-Ed. https://www.psy-ed.com/wpblog/setting-limits-for-children/

30. UNICEF. (n.d.). How to communicate effectively with your young child. UNICEF Parenting. https://www.unicef.org/parenting/child-care/9-tips-for-b etter-communication

31. University of Washington Medicine. (2022, May 10). Youth mental health is poor. Active listening can help. Right as Rain by UW Medicine. https://rightas rain.uwmedicine.org/life/parenthood/active-listening-skills

32. WebMD. (n.d.). Breathing techniques for stress relief. WebMD. https://ww w.webmd.com/balance/stress-management/stress-relief-breathing-techniques

About the author

Claudia Turcotte is an inspiring mother of two who is deeply passionate about her work as an emotional wellness coach and author.

With years of experience in the field of emotional health, Claudia is a dedicated advocate for mental well-being, focusing on helping individuals and families navigate the complexities of their emotions.

She is committed to providing practical strategies and insights that are easy to implement and highly effective. With her extensive knowledge and experience, Claudia is now channeling it into this book on emotional wellness for parents and family, offering guidance on managing stress, anger, and other challenging emotions.

Claudia's mission is to make emotional wellness accessible and achievable for everyone, regardless of their background. Her goal is to help as many people as possible understand and manage their emotions, leading to healthier and happier lives.

Her enthusiasm and passion for emotional wellness are inspiring, and her forthcoming book is set to become an essential resource for those looking to improve their emotional health and build stronger, more resilient relationships.